AMERICA'S HAUNTED HOUSES
PUBLIC AND PRIVATE

AMERICA'S
HAUNTED HOUSES
PUBLIC AND PRIVATE

HANS HOLZER

By the author of Ghost Hunter, Yankee Ghosts and Murder in Amityville.

LONGMEADOW PRESS

CONTENTS

FOREWORD

merica's Haunted Houses are no less interesting nor their stories any less dramatic than those of houses in such traditional ghost countries as England or Ireland. American ghosts, after all, are plain Americans who somehow got into emotional turmoil at death, and cannot adjust.

Whenever I am called upon to help solve a case of this kind, usually by the owners of a house who want to restore their own tranquillity and sometimes also because they want to give peace to the restless wraiths, I do so willingly if I feel there is evidence to back up the claims.

One must always rule out ordinary causes of strange noises before assuming they are ghostly manifestations, and I also want to know who my witnesses are in respect to their background, reliability and, yes, mental state, so as not to be accused by potential critics of being gullible or less than objective and scientific in my work.

Having determined that there is, in fact, a haunting, I will return with a competent trance medium, such as the late Ethel Johnson Myers or Sybil Leek, or nowadays, Yolana Lassaw. In deep trance and under my direction and control, the alleged ghost will use the medium's body to speak to me, and under my questioning disclose facts about his or her identity and problems. At the end of such an often difficult session, I will explain the ghost's true condition, so as to free the entity from the compulsion of "staying on" where no further need to do so exists. Ghosts are rarely aware of the passage of time and change of circumstances, and need to be helped in this respect. Ghosts do not leave the immediate area of their passing, do not travel, and cannot harm anyone.

The methods I use are standard procedure in parapsychology and require academic training and understanding. Amateur "investigators" can do more damage than good at times, especially when they travel as "demonologists" looking for demons and devils as the cause of a haunting. There is nothing out there that isn't human, and real help can only come by dealing dispassionately with such occurrences.

Lastly, one should also keep in mind that of all the reported sightings of ghostly manifestations, or auditory phenomena, only a small percentage are "true" ghosts in the sense that they are caused by human beings cut off from reality by untimely or tragic deaths, seeking answers to their panic. A much larger percentage of such experiences are so-called psychic impressions, or replays of past events, which any gifted psychic or even many ordinary people who are sensitive enough to "pick it up" will relive.

The cases reported in this work, however, are not psychic impressions, but honest-to-goodness *ghosts*.

Those seeking help with their own hauntings may write to me in care of my publishers. I expect a television series based on my work with ghosts and hauntings to be done before long, so that even more of the public can learn the truth about hauntings, and need neither be afraid, nor unduly alarmed, if they happen to have a ghost in the house!

Hans Holzer, Ph.D.

INTRODUCTION

ne of the things my readers should keep in mind when looking at these pages is the need to forget a popular notion about ghosts: that they are dangerous, fearful and can hurt people. Nothing could be further from the truth. Nor are ghosts the figment of imagination, or the product of motion picture writers. Ghostly experiences are neither supernatural nor unnatural, but fit into the general pattern of the universe we live in, although the majority of conventional scientists has not yet understood what exactly ghosts are. Some have, and those who have studied parapsychology have come to understand that human life does continue beyond what we commonly call death. Once in a while, there are extraordinary circumstances when death occurs, and these exceptional circumstances create what we popularly call ghosts and haunted houses.

Ever since the dawn of mankind, people have believed in ghosts. The fear of the unknown, the certainty that there was something somewhere out there, bigger than life, beyond its pale, and more powerful than anything walking the earth, has persisted throughout the ages. It had its origins in primitive man's thinking. To him, there were good and evil forces at work in nature, both ruled over by supernatural beings, and to some degree capable of being influenced by the attitudes and prayers of man. The fear of death was, of course, one of the strongest human emotions. It still is. Although some belief in survival after physical death has existed from the beginning of time, no one ever cherished the notion of leaving this earth. Thus, death represented a menace.

Then what are ghosts—if indeed there *are* such things? To the materialist and the professional skeptic—that is to say, people who do not wish to be disturbed in their belief that death is the end of life as we know it—the notion of ghosts is unacceptable. No matter how much evidence is presented for the reality of the phenomena, they will argue against it and ascribe it to any of several "natural"

causes. Either delusion or hallucination must be the explanation, or perhaps a mirage, if not outright trickery on the part of parties unknown. Entire professional groups who deal in the manufacture of illusions have taken it upon themselves to label anything that defies their ability to reproduce it artificially through trickery or manipulation, as false or nonexistent. Especially among photographers and magicians, the notion that ghosts exist has never been a popular one. But authentic reports of psychic phenomena along ghostly lines keep coming into reputable report centers such as the various societies for psychic research, or to parapsychologists like myself.

Granted, a certain number of these reports may be due to inaccurate reporting, self-delusion, or other errors of fact. Still there remains an impressive number of cases that cannot be explained by any other means than that of extrasensory perception.

What exactly is a ghost? In terms of psychic research, a ghost appears to be a surviving emotional memory of someone who has died traumatically, and usually tragically, but is unaware of his or her death. A few ghosts may realize that they are dead but are confused as to where they are, or why they do not feel quite the way they used to feel. When death occurs unexpectedly or unacceptably, or when a person has lived in a place for a very long time, acquiring certain routine habits and becoming very attached to the premises, sudden, unexpected death may come as a shock. Unwilling to part with the physical world, such human personalities then continue to stay on in the very spot where their tragedy or their emotional attachment had existed prior to physical death.

Ghosts do not travel; they do not follow people home; nor do they appear at more than one place. Nevertheless, there are also reliable reports of the apparitions of the dead having indeed travelled and appeared to several people in various locations. Those, however, are not ghosts in the sense I understand the term. They are free spirits, or discarnate entities, who are inhabiting what Dr. Joseph B. Rhine of Duke University has called the "world of the mind." They may be attracted for emotional reasons to one or the other place at a given moment in order to communicate with someone on the earth plane. But a true ghost is unable to make such moves freely. Ghosts by their very nature are not unlike psychotics in the flesh; they are quite unable to understand fully their own predicament. They are kept in place, both in time and space, *by* their emotional ties to the spot. Nothing can pry them loose from it so long as they are reliving over and over again in their minds the events leading to their unhappy deaths.

Sometimes this is difficult for the ghost, as he may be too strongly attached to feelings of guilt or revenge to "let go." But eventually a combination of informative remarks by the parapsychologist and suggestions to call upon the deceased person's family will pry him loose and send him out into the free world of spirit.

Ghosts have never harmed anyone except through fear found within the witness, of his own doing and because of his own ignorance as to what ghosts represent. In the few cases where ghosts have attacked people of flesh and blood, such as the ghostly abbot of Trondheim, it is simply a matter of mistaken identity, where extreme violence at the time of death has left a strong residue of memory in the individual ghosts. By and large, it is entirely safe to be a ghost hunter or to become a witness to phenomena of this kind.

In his chapter on ghosts, in *Man, Myth, and Magic*, Douglas Hill presents alternate hypotheses one by one and examines them. Having done so, he states, "None of these explanations is wholly satisfactory, for none seems applicable to the whole range of ghost lore." Try as man might, ghosts can't be explained away, nor will they disappear. They continue to appear frequently all over the world, to young and old, rich and poor, in old houses and in new houses, on airports and in streets, and wherever tragedy strikes man. For ghosts are indeed nothing more or nothing less than a human being trapped by special circumstances in this world while already being of the next. Or, to put it another way, human beings whose spirit is unable to leave the earthly surroundings because of unfinished business or emotional entanglements.

But even if you do not encounter ghosts or have a psychic experience in the houses described here, you will find them fascinating places. As an adventure in historical research, haunted houses have no equal.

Lastly, I would suggest to my readers not to get into arguments about the existence or nonexistence of ghosts and haunted houses. Everyone must find their own explanations for what they experience, and *belief* has nothing to do with it. Belief is the uncritical acceptance of something you cannot prove one way or another, and the evidence for ghosts and hauntings is so overwhelming, so large and so well documented, that arguing the existence of the evidence would be a foolish thing indeed. While there may be various explanations for what people experience in haunted houses, no explanation will ever be sufficient to negate the experiences themselves. Thus, if you are one of the many who enter a haunted house and have a genuine experience in it, be assured that you are a perfectly normal human being, who uses a natural gift, which is neither harmful nor dangerous but may in the long run be informative and even useful. Good hunting.

Hans Holzer, Ph.D.

1
THE GHOSTLY ADMIRAL

he J. family has a lovely summer home at Whitefield, New Hampshire. The house stands in a secluded part of the forest at the end of a narrow winding driveway lined by tall trees, and there is a wooden porch around it on three sides. The house itself rises up three stories and is painted white in the usual New England manner.

The house was called "Miz'n Top" by its original owner and builder, an Admiral. I questioned E.J., who was on the Goddard College faculty as an instructor, about his experiences in the old house.

"When my parents decided to turn the attic into a club room where I could play with my friends," E.J. began, "they cut windows into the wall and threw out all the possessions of the former owner of the house they had found there. I was about seven at the time.

"Soon after, footsteps and other noises began to be heard in the attic and along the corridors and stairs leading toward it. But it wasn't until the summer of 1955 that I experienced my first really important disturbance. That summer we slept here for the first time in this room, one flight up, and almost nightly we were either awakened by noises or could not sleep, waiting for them to begin. At first we thought they were animal noises, but they were too much like footsteps and heavy objects being moved across the floor overhead, and down the hall. We were so scared we refused to move in our beds or turn down the lights."

"But you did know of the tradition that the house was haunted, did you not?" I asked.

"Yes, I grew up with it. All I knew is what I had heard from my parents. The original owner and builder of the house, an admiral named Hawley, and his wife, were both most difficult people. The admiral died in 1933. In 1935 the house was sold by his daughter, who was then living in Washington, to my parents. Anyone who happened to be trespassing on his territory would be chased off it, and I imagine he would not have liked our throwing out his sea chest and other personal possessions."

"Any other experience outside the footsteps?"

"About four years ago," E.J. replied, "my wife and I, and a neighbor, S.V., were sitting in the living room downstairs discussing interpretations of the Bible. I needed a dictionary at one point in the discussion and got up to fetch it from upstairs.

"I ran up to the bend here, in front of this room, and there were no lights on at the time. I opened the door to the club room and started to go up the stairs, when suddenly I walked into what I can only describe as a *warm, wet blanket,* something that touched me physically as if it had been hung from wires in the corridor. I was very upset, backed out and went downstairs. My wife took one look at me and said, 'you're white.' 'I know,' I said. 'I think I just walked into the admiral.'"

"Has anyone else had an encounter with a ghost here?" I asked.

"Well another house guest went up into the attic and came running down reporting that the door knob had turned in front of his very eyes before he could reach for it to open the door. The dog was with him, and steadfastly refused to cross the threshold. Another house guest arrived very late at night, about five years ago. We had already gone to bed, and he knew he had to sleep in the attic since every other room was already taken. Instead, I found him sleeping in the living room, on the floor, in the morning. He knew nothing about the ghost. 'I'm not going back up there any more,' he vowed, and would not say anything further. I guess he must have run into the admiral."

Every member of the family had at one time or another had an encounter with the ghostly admiral, it appeared. Sybil Leek, my mediumistic friend, had come with us and soon she was able to pick up the vibrations of the unseen visitor. As soon as she had gone into a trance state she made contact with the admiral. She even had the name right, although she had not been present when I had spoken to the owners of the house earlier! It seemed that the admiral had resented the new owners throwing out all of his things. He did not like the house having been sold the way it was, but would have preferred it to go to his son. I implored the ghostly admiral not to upset the family now living in the house and he replied, in rather a stiff navy manner, that he was a tidy person and would take care of himself. When we left Whitefield, it seems to me that the old sea dog must have felt a lot better; after all, how many New Yorkers would drive all the way up to New Hampshire to talk to him after all those years?

The house is in private hands. I would not suggest dropping in on them, however, because privacy is a very precious thing, especially in New England.

The former owner of this New Hampshire house, a retired Admiral, never really left: someone even walked "into" his ghost!

2
THE GHOSTLY GUARDIAN OF THE ADOBE

n adobe is a Spanish-Colonial house, a style fairly common in southern California. Adobe houses were popular among eighteenth century Spanish settlers, because of the economics of building them, and the ease of making them pleasant to the eye.

The *Casa Alvarado* is probably California's best preserved adobe house, one of the few Spanish houses still standing and inhabited by people descended from the original settlers who had come there with Don Gaspar de Portola and Padre Junitero Serra in 1769. It stands on a piece of land which was once the property of two proud Spanish gentlemen who received it jointly in a Mexican land grant in 1837. The famous historical house then was owned by a variety of owners until it passed back into the Alvarado family again a few years ago, when the family did everything in their power to restore it to its original appearance. A little to the south of the house there was once a wooden barn, part of the estate. The barn, dating back to the 1840's had long since been turned into a house. Though owned by different people, it is connected to the adobe, standing on the same piece of land.

When I visited the barn, now a pleasant house, it was owned by the L. family. They were not particularly interested in ghosts, but it turned out that they had little choice. Shortly after the L.'s had moved into the converted barn, the first event took place. A Mexican lady named Mrs. N. was cleaning upstairs; she was alone. Suddenly, she clearly heard footsteps coming toward her, but there was no one to be seen, yet the floorboards reverberated with the weight of a person, quite heavy apparently, rushing past her. Immediately she ran out of the house.

The Mexican lady was afraid to tell her employer about this incident, but she need not have worried about it. Mrs. L. soon knew that there was someone other than the family living in the house with them. In February of the same year, she found herself in the house with her two girls, while her husband had gone out to attend to his income tax report. The girls, then aged ten and twelve, were in the kitchen with her that evening, when she clearly heard heavy footsteps upstairs.

This was immediately followed by the sound of someone opening and closing various drawers, and of doors being violently opened and slammed shut. It sounded as if someone were very angry at not finding what he was looking for, and frantically going from room to room searching for something.

Mrs. L. did not feel up to going it alone, so she just sat there and waited. For a full ten minutes, the racket went on upstairs. Then it stopped as abruptly as it had begun. About half an hour later, her sister-in-law Doris and her son's fiancé, Marion, arrived at the house. Reinforced by her relatives, Mrs. L. finally dared go upstairs. From the sound of the commotion she was sure to find various drawers open and doors jammed. But when she entered the rooms upstairs, she found everything completely untouched by human hands.

A few days later, Mrs. L. and her husband were having coffee in the kitchen downstairs. It was a clear, sunny afternoon and all seemed peaceful and quiet. Denise, the elder daughter, was upstairs, sitting at her window seat and reading a

When the owners made structural changes in this California house, the ghost of a previous owner resented it. . . . and let them know.

book. For a moment, she took her eyes off the book, for it had seemed to her that a slight breeze had disturbed the atmosphere of the room. She was right, for she saw a large man walk across the room and enter the large walk-in closet at the other end of it. She assumed it was her father, of course, and asked what he was looking for. When she received no reply, she got up and went to the closet herself. It struck her funny that the closet door was closed. She opened it, wondering if her father was perhaps playing games with her. The closet was empty. Terrified, she rushed downstairs.

Soon afterward, the two girls woke up in the middle of the night even though they were usually very sound sleepers. The time was two A.M. and there was sufficient light in the room for them to distinguish the figure of a large man in black standing by their beds! He seemed to stare down at them without moving. They let out a scream almost in unison, bringing their parents up the stairs. By that time, the apparition had dissolved.

The war of nerves continued, however. A few nights later, the girls' screams attracted the parents and when they raced upstairs they found the girls barricaded inside the room, holding the door as if someone were trying to force it open!

For a moment, the parents could clearly see that some unseen force was balancing the door against the weight of the two young girls on the other side of it—then it slacked and fell shut. Almost hysterical with panic now, the girls explained, between sobs, that someone had tried to enter their room, that they had wakened and sensed it and pushed against the door—only to find the force outside getting stronger momentarily. Had the parents not arrived on the scene at this moment, the door would have been pushed open and whatever it was that did this, would have entered the bedroom.

But the door did not stop the black, shadowy intruder from entering that room. On several occasions, the girls saw him standing by their bedside and when they fully woke and jumped out of bed, he disappeared.

The L.'s finally received an answer to their problem.

A famous psychic lady walked through their house and immediately felt its hostile atmosphere.

"Something threatens this house," she mumbled, "and it has to do with both houses and the land, not just this house."

Suddenly it occurred to the L.'s that their troubles had started only when they had decided to make major structural changes in the house.

"Aha," the lady psychic said, "there is your problem."

After this, the L.'s proceeded with greater caution in their plans to change the house. Perhaps the question of their justified improvements having been openly discussed somehow reassured the unseen ears of the guardian.

3
THE GHOST
AT THE ALTAR

onsidering that churches and religion in general should give a man peace of mind, it comes perhaps as a surprise to some of my readers that even churches can be haunted by ghosts. But those who serve religion—priests, ministers and rabbis—are, after all, also human beings who may undergo emotional problems and stress. Such was the case in a large and very beautiful church not far from Pittsburgh, Pennsylvania.

About an hour's drive from Pittsburgh, in the small town of Millvale, hard by the Allegheny River, stands an imposing stone church built at the turn of the last century. Positioned as it is on a bluff looking down toward the river, it seems somewhat out of place for so small a town as Millvale. Attached to the building is a school and rectory, and there is an air of clean efficiency about the entire complex. This is a Roman Catholic church, and the priests are all of Yugoslav background. Thus there is a peculiarity about the ritual, about the atmosphere inside the church, and about the men who serve here. The church is very large, and the altar is framed by original paintings in the Yugoslav style. They are the work of Maxim Hvatka, the celebrated Yugoslav artist who worked in the early part of this century and who died a few years ago. Near the altar there was a large eternal light—that is to say, an enclosed candle protected from drafts or other interference. This is important, since much of the phenomenon centers in this area and includes the blowing out of the eternal light by unknown causes.

Although the administrators of the church do not exactly cherish the notion that they have a ghost, there have been a number of witnesses who have seen a figure pass by the altar. The painter Hvatka himself saw the ghostly apparition while working on his frescoes. Chills, which could not be accounted for, were also noted in the immediate area of the eternal light.

There is nothing concerning the present-day church that would account for the apparition of a figure at the altar. However, prior to the erection of the present church, a wooden church had stood on the same spot. It was Father Ranzinger who had built the wooden church, and who had devoted most of his life to that church and its flock. One night, the wooden church went up in flames. Father Ranzinger's lifework was destroyed. I suspect that it is his ghost that has been seen.

After a while I was able to convince the priest who had admitted me to the church, that I meant no harm to the reputation and good name of the church and this particular order of priests, but that I was only interested in writing about natural psychic phenomena, which, after all, are part of God's world. Father X, as he insisted on being called, readily admitted that I was telling the truth and with a somewhat enigmatic smile, he admitted that he, too, had had psychic experiences all his life. As we went on talking, he admitted further that he had seen the ghost of the departed priest himself as had a painter who had been employed in the building to restore the magnificent frescoes put there years before. Strangely enough, the only one other than myself who wrote anything at all about the haunted church at Millvale was none other than the famous Yugoslav author Louis Adamic, a self-confessed agnostic, a man who does not feel that there is any way to *know* that God exists. As for the ghostly priest at the altar, he must still be there, roaming the church at will. In view of the difficulties of getting into the church in the first place, I was unable to bring a medium there to attempt a release of the unhappy priest. Thus, my friends, if you happen to be near Pittsburgh and feel like visiting the haunted church of Millvale, and if the time is just right, perhaps at dusk or at dawn, you may just encounter the restless ghost of Father Ranzinger. That is, if he hasn't long since faded away and come to peace with himself, as well he should.

4

BENEDICT ARNOLD'S GHOSTLY FRIEND

p near the town of Hudson, New York, in the open countryside, there stands a lovely Colonial house owned by a certain Mrs. C., a teacher by profession, a quiet and reserved lady who had had a visual experience with a ghost in the attic of her old house. I visited the house in the company of medium Ethel Johnson Meyers on a winter afternoon. Because of its isolation one had the feeling of being far out in the country, when in fact the thruway connecting New York with Albany passes a mere ten minutes away. The house is gleaming white, or nearly so, for the ravages of time have taken their toll. Mr. and Mrs. C. bought it twenty years prior to our visit, but after divorcing Mr. C., she was unable to keep it up as it should have been, and gradually the interior especially fell into a state of disrepair. The outside still showed its noble past, such as the columned entrance, the Grecian influence in the construction of the roof, and the beautiful Colonial shutters.

Five months after she had moved into the house she was looking through the attic, even though she had been told that the previous owner had sold everything in the house at auction. She found an old trunk and when she opened it and rummaged through it she discovered a little waistcoat, a hat and a peculiar bonnet, the kind that used to be worn before 1800. At first she thought it had belonged to a child but then she realized it was for a small adult. As Mrs. C. was standing there, fascinated by the material, she became aware out of the corner of her eye of a pinpoint of light. Her first thought was, I must tell Jim that there is a hole in the roof where this light is coming through. But she kept looking and, being preoccupied with the material in the trunk, paid no attention to the light. Something, however, made her look up, and she noticed that the light had now become substantially larger. Also, it was coming nearer, changing its position all the time. The phenomenon began to fascinate her. She wasn't thinking of ghosts or psychic phenomena at all, merely wondering what this was all about. As the

This lovely pre-revolutionary house near Hudson, N.Y. still has its owner trying to clear his friend Benedict Arnold's name . . . his ghost won't leave because of it.

light came nearer and nearer, she suddenly thought, why, that looks like a human figure!

Eventually, it stopped near the trunk, and Mrs. C. realized it was a human figure, the *figure of an elderly lady*. She was unusually small and delicate and wore the very bonnet Mrs. C. had discovered at the bottom of the trunk! The woman's clothes seemed gray, and Mrs. C. noticed the apron the woman was wearing. As she watched the ghostly apparition in fascinated horror, the little lady used her apron in a movement that is generally used in the country to shoo away the chickens. However, the motion was directed against *her*, as if the apparition wanted to shoo her away from "her" trunk!

Soon I had medium Ethel Johnson Meyers seated in one of the chairs, ready to slip into trance. But instead of a lady claiming her possessions from the trunk, we were faced with a gentleman straight out of the eighteenth century. He said he was waiting for General Horatio Gates. The general had promised him to come and he wouldn't budge until the general appeared. But the ghost became more and more agitated, calling for "Ben" to help him. Crying out for Benedict Arnold and assuring us that he was a loyal subject, made things even more confusing until the medium's control personality, Albert, spoke to us, explaining things.

"He gives false names. As far as we can judge here, he believes he was hanged. He was a Loyalist, refusing to take refuge with Americans. He didn't pose as a Revolutionary until the very end, when he thought he could be saved." Albert explained that this had taken place in this house during the Revolutionary War. I asked Albert if he could tell us anything further about the woman who was seen in the house.

"She passed here and remained simply because she wanted to watch her husband's struggles to save himself from being dishonored and discredited. Her husband is the one who was speaking to you."

I asked Gus K. of the local Chamber of Commerce, to comment. "Benedict Arnold was brought to this area after the battle of Saratoga to recuperate for one or two nights," Kramer explained. General Arnold, long before he turned traitor to the American cause, had been a very successful field commander and administrative officer on the side of the Revolution. "He spent the night in the Kinderhook area," Gus continued. "The location of the house itself is not definitely known, but it is known that he spent the night here. Horatio Gates, who was the American leader in the battle of Saratoga, also spent several nights in the immediate area. It is not inconceivable that this place, which was a mansion in those days, might have entertained these men at the time."

"What about the hanging?"

"Seven Tories were hanged in this area during the Revolutionary War. Some of the greatest fighting took place here, and it is quite conceivable that something took place at this old mansion. Again, it completely bears out what Mrs. Meyers spoke of while in trance."

I asked Gus to pinpoint the period for me. "This would have been in 1777, toward October or November."

The house is still privately owned, but with some luck you might be able to arrange for a visit beforehand.

5

THE HAUNTED ROCKING CHAIR AT ASH LAWN

N ot only houses are haunted, even furniture can be the recipient of ghostly attention. Not very far from Castle Hill, Virginia is one of America's most important historical buildings, the country home once owned by James Monroe where he and Thomas Jefferson often exchanged conversation and also may have made some very big political decisions in their time. Today this is a modest appearing cottage, rather than a big manor house, and it is well kept. It may be visited by tourists at certain hours, since it is considered an historical shrine. If any of my readers are in the area and feel like visiting Ash Lawn, I would suggest they do not mention ghosts too openly with the guides or caretakers.

Actually the ghostly goings-on center around a certain wooden rocking chair in the main room. This has been seen to rock without benefit of human hands. I don't know how many people have actually seen the chair rock, but Mrs. J. Massey, who lived in the area for many years, has said to me when I visited the place, "I will tell anyone and I have no objection to its being known, that I've seen not once but time and time again the rocking chair rocking exactly as though someone were in it. My brother John has seen it too. Whenever we touched it it would stop rocking."

This house, though small and cozy, nevertheless was James Monroe's favorite house even after he moved to the bigger place which became his stately home later on in his career. At Ash Lawn he could get away from his affairs of state, away from public attention, to discuss matters of great concern with his friend Thomas Jefferson who lived only two miles away at Monticello.

Who is the ghost in the rocking chair? Perhaps it is only a spirit, not an earthbound ghost, a spirit who has become so attached to his former home and refuge from the affairs of state, that he still likes to sit now and then in his own rocking chair thinking things over.

This chair at Ash Lawn rocks by its own volition at times . . . possibly because President James Monroe, the owner, still likes to sit in it now and then.

6

THE LITTLE OLD LADY GHOST ON BANK STREET

What I'm about to relate to you happened in 1957, but the house is still there, and perhaps even the owners haven't changed. It was then a private house and it still is now.

At the time when I became involved with it, or rather with the ghost in it, it belonged to Dr. Harvey S., an engineer by profession, and his wife, an artist, who is an Osage Indian. The house in which they lived was then 125 years old, made of red brick, and still in excellent condition.

Digging into the past of their home, the S.'s established that a Mrs. M. had run the house as a nineteen-room boarding establishment for years before selling it to them. However, Mrs. M. wasn't of much help when questioned. She knew nothing of her predecessors.

After the S.'s had acquired the house, and the other tenants had finally left, they did the house over. The downstairs became one long living room, extending from front to back, adorned by a fireplace and a number of good paintings and ceramics. In the back part of this room, the S.'s placed a heavy wooden table. The rear door led to a small garden, and a narrow staircase led to the second floor.

During quiet moments, they often thought they heard a woman's footsteps on the staircase, sometimes crossing the upper floors, sometimes a sound like a light hammering. Strangely enough, the sounds were heard more often in the daytime than at night, a habit most unbecoming a traditional haunt. The S.'s were never frightened by this. They simply went to investigate what might have caused the

The ashes of a lady killed crossing the street in front of #11 Bank Street were hidden in this house—and her restless spirit demanded she be buried in hallowed ground.

noises, but never found any visible evidence. There was no "rational" explanation for them, either. One Sunday in January of 1957, they decided to clock the noises, and found that the ghostly goings-on lasted all day; during these hours, they would run upstairs to trap the trespasser—only to find empty rooms and corridors. Calling out to the unseen brought no reply, either. An English carpenter by the name of Arthur B. was as well adjusted to reality as are the S.'s, but he also heard the footsteps. His explanation that "one hears all sorts of noises in old houses" did not help matters any. Sadie, the maid, heard the noises too, and after an initial period of panic, got accustomed to them as if they were part of the house's routine—which indeed they were!

One morning in February, Arthur B. was working in a room on the top floor, hammering away at the ceiling. He was standing on a stepladder that allowed him to just about touch the ceiling. Suddenly, plaster and dust showered down on his head, and something heavy fell and hit the floor below. Mrs. S. in her first-floor bedroom heard the thump. Before she could investigate the source of the loud noise, there was Brodie at her door, saying: "It's me, Ma'am. I'm leaving the job! I've found the body!" But he was being facetious. What he actually found was a black-painted metal container about twice the size of a coffee can. On it there was a partially faded label, reading *"The last remains of Elizabeth Bullock, deceased. Cremated January 21, 1931."* The label also bore the imprint of the United States Crematory Company, Ltd., Middle Village, Borough of Queens, New York, and stamped on the top of the can was the number—37251.

Curiously, the ceiling that had hidden the container dated back at least to 1880, which was long before Elizabeth Bullock had died. One day, the frail woman crossed Hudson Street, a few blocks from the S.'s residence. A motorist going at full speed saw her too late, and she was run over. Helpful hands carried her to a nearby drugstore, while other bystanders called for an ambulance. But help arrived too late for Mrs. Bullock. She died at the drugstore before any medical help arrived. Strangely enough, when Dr. S. looked through the records, he found that Mrs. Bullock had never lived at 11 Bank Street at all!

Still, Mrs. Bullock's ashes were found in that house. How to explain that? In the crematory's books, her home address was listed at 113 Perry Street. Dr. S. called on Charles Dominick, the undertaker in the case. His place of business had been on West 11th Street, not far from Bank Street.

Upon invitation by the owners of the house I arranged for a seance with the help of medium Ethel Johnson Meyers and on July 17, 1957 we tried to make contact with the restless spirit of Mrs. Bullock. We then realized why Mrs. Bullock could not find peace and didn't mind hanging around Bank Street for the time being, where, after all, her ashes were being kept. She married out of the faith, she explained to the medium, and in those days that was a serious breach of family tradition. It was her husband who had stolen the ashes and hidden them in a near-by house, and when repairs were made in that house the cannister was stashed away where no one was likely to find it. But what now, I asked the ghost. What would she like us to do with the ashes. The ghost was adamant about being buried with her own family. Her mother would not forgive her for having married a man outside the Roman Catholic faith. But being buried in a Presbyterian cemetery, to please her late husband, would not do either, because it might upset *her* family. Then what, I demanded to know. But the solution came from the owners of the house, not from the ghost. A simple grave was arranged for the late Mrs. Bullock in the backyard, with an equally simple non-denomination cross above it. And there the ghost, and the story rests.

7
THE GHOSTS
IN THE
BASEMENT

ary lives in Atlanta, Georgia, a quiet women who speaks with a charming southern accent and is rather conservative in her way of life. Even her special talent of being able to read the tarot cards for her friends used to be an embarrassment to her because of her religion and because of what the neighbors might say if they found out, not to mention the fact that everyone would want a reading from her.

At the time I met her she had two lovely daughters, Katie, a 15-year-old, and Boots, who went to college. On the day of Halloween, 1962, she and her girls had moved into an attractive 18-year-old house in Atlanta. It stood in a quiet suburban neighborhood amid other small homes of no particular distinction. Not far from the house are the tracks of a railroad which is nowadays used only for freight. Famous old Fort McPherson is not far away; during the Civil War one of the bloodiest engagements was fought on this spot.

The house has two levels; at street level, there is a large living room which one enters from the front side of the house, then there are three bedrooms and on the right side of the house, a den leading into a kitchen. From one of the bedrooms a stair secured by an iron railing leads into the basement. There is a closet underneath the stairs. In back of the house there is a large patio and there are also outside stairs leading again into the basement. Only the right-hand third of the basement area is actually used by the family, a laundry room occupies most of the space and a wall seals it off from the undeveloped "dirt" area of the basement.

The house itself feels cozy and warm, the furniture is pleasant and functional, and if it weren't for some unusual events that had occurred in the house, one might never suspect it of being anything but just another ordinary suburban home.

Soon after they had moved in, Mary and her daughters knew there was something very odd about the house. She would wake up in the middle of the night because she heard someone digging down in the basement. She thought this entirely out of the question, but when the noise persisted night after night, she was wondering whether the neighbors might be putting in a water pipe. After a while, she decided to find out who was doing the digging. She left her bed and went downstairs, but there was nothing to be seen. There were no rats or mice which could have caused the strange noise. There was no freshly turned up dirt either. The neighbors weren't doing any digging. Even more mysterious, Mary and her two daughters kept hearing the noise of someone trying to break into the house, always at 2:00 in the morning. And when they checked there was never anyone there. They called the police but the police failed to turn up any clues. Mary installed heavy bolts inside the front and rear doors, but the day she returned from an errand to an empty house she found the heavy bolts ripped away by unseen hands.

At that time Mary was estranged from her doctor husband, and she was afraid to discuss the strange phenomena with him, since he put no stock into psychic phenomena and might have taken advantage of the information to have Mary declared in need of psychiatric treatment. Mary was in the habit of taking afternoon naps but now her naps kept being disturbed by an unseen person entering the house, walking through it as if he or she knew it well, and sometimes even running the water or flushing the toilet! Often, when she was doing her laundry in the basement she would clearly hear footsteps overhead then the sound of drawers being opened and shut and water being run. But when she checked, there was no one about and nothing had changed.

At first she kept the disturbing news from her daughters but soon she discovered that the children had also heard the strange noises. In addition, Katie had felt a pair of hands on her during the night when she knew she was alone in her room. Even in plain daylight such heavy objects as books began to disappear and reappear in other places as if someone were trying to play a game with them. At that time Boots, the older girl, was at college and when she came back from school she had no idea what her sister and mother had been through recently in the house. So it was a shock for her to hear someone using a typewriter in the basement when they all knew that there was no one there and no typewriter in the house. The family held a conference and it was decided that what they had in the house was a ghost, or perhaps several. By now they had gotten used to the idea, however, and it did not frighten them as much as before.

One night Katie was asleep when she awoke with the feeling that she was not alone. As she opened her eyes she saw standing by her bedside a shadowy figure. Since her mother was in the other bedroom, she knew that it could not have been her.

Soon, Mary and her girls realized that they weren't dealing with just one ghost. On several occasions they quick footsteps of a child were also heard along with the heavier footsteps of an adult. Then someone seemed to be calling out to them by name. One day in January of 1968 when they had gotten accustomed to their unseen visitors Mary awoke to the sound of music coming from the kitchen area. She investigated this at once but found neither a radio nor any other reason for the music that could be accepted on a rational basis. She returned to bed and tried to ignore it. Just then two sets of footfalls reached her ears right through the covers. One set of feet seemed to turn toward her daughter Katie's room, while the other pair of feet came right toward her bed, where they stopped. Something ice cold then seemed to touch her. She screamed in fear and jumped from her bed and this apparently broke the phenomenon and again there was no one about.

Mary began to wonder who was the person in the household who made the phenomenon possible, because she knew enough about psychic phenomena to realize that someone had to be the medium. One night she received the answer. She awakened to the sound of a voice coming from her daughter Katie's room. A female voice was saying a phrase over and over and Katie was answering by repeating it. She could clearly hear, "golden sand" spoken in a sweet, kindly voice and her daughter Katie repeating it in a childish voice totally different from her normal adult tone. Then she heard Katie clap her hands and say, "Now what can I do?" When Mary entered Katie's room she saw her daughter fast asleep. When questioned the next day about the incident, Katie remembered absolutely nothing. But the incidents continued.

One day Katie saw a woman in her 40s, and felt someone fondling her hair. It seemed a kind gesture and Katie was not afraid. By now Mary wondered whether she herself might not be the person to whom the phenomena occurred rather than just her daughter. She had always had psychic ability so she decided to test this potential mediumship within her. Relaxing deeply in an effort to find out who the ghost was and what the ghost wanted in the house, Mary was able to hear with her inner voice the psychic message sent out from the woman. Over and over again she heard the phrase spoken within her – "I need your help to cross the stream!" Several days later she heard the same female voice whisper in her ear, "I need your help!" "Where are you?" Mary said aloud. "In the basement, in the dirt," the voice answered. Soon Mary realized there was another ghost in the house, this one male. Mary woke from an afternoon nap because she heard someone come through the front door. She sat up and yelled at the unseen presence to go away and leave her alone. But a man's gruff voice answered her. "She can see me!" But Mary did not see anyone. Still, she became more and more convinced that the man was angry at her for having paid attention to the female ghost and Mary wondered whether the two of them had a connection. Mary called on sincere friends to form a "psychic rescue circle," that is to try to make contact with the restless ghosts and, if possible, send them away. It didn't help. Soon after, Mary heard the pleading voice again, "I need you. Come to the basement." Mary then went to the basement where she said a prayer for the departed. Whether the prayer did it, or whether the ghosts had finally realized that they were staying on in a house that belonged to another time, there were no further disturbances after that.

8
MISS BOYD OF CHARLES STREET, MANHATTAN

ne of the oldest and historically most interesting sections of New York City is Greenwich Village, where many houses dating back to the early nineteenth, eighteenth, and even seventeenth century still exist. The people living in them sometimes have to share the appointments with an unseen entity or even a seen one, but ghosts and old houses seem to go together and those among the people living in this part of New York whom I have interviewed over the years because of ghostly manifestations have never thought that there was anything remarkably horrible about them. If anything they were curious about the person or persons they shared their houses with.

Some years ago I had the pleasure of meeting a certain Miss Boyd down on Charles Street and the meeting was mutually useful. Miss Boyd of course was a ghost. All of this happened because Barrie, a friend, had taken an apartment on Charles Street, and found that his ground floor apartment contained a ghost. Halloween, 1964, I visited the apartment in the company of medium Sybil Leek, and I had no idea whom I might meet there apart from the flesh and blood people then occupying the apartment. There was a fire in the fireplace and an appropriate wind howling outside, but it was novelist Elizabeth B., Barrie's friend, who set the proper mood. She explained that the whole thing started when one of Barrie's house guests, Adriana, had been awakened in bed by a rather violent push of her arm. At the same time she felt herself compelled to burst into tears and wept profusely, although there was no reason for it. Somehow she partook of another person's feelings, involving a great deal of sorrow. This happened several nights in a row. However, Adriana did not tell Barrie about it. There really was no need to, because one night he arrived around 1:00 in the morning to find Adriana practically drowning in her tears. When his house guest left, he tried to dismiss the whole thing, but he, too, felt a "presence" watching him all the time. On one occasion, he saw a whitish mist, and was sure that someone was looking at him.

Sybil Leek felt that communication with the unseen entity was possible. Gradually falling deeper and deeper into a trance state, she made contact with the unhappy woman who could not leave the spot of much suffering in her own lifetime. "Her name is Boyd," Sybil explained and then the entity, the ghost herself, took over Sybil's speech mechanism and I was able to question her about her grievances. Apparently Miss Boyd was looking for a document having to do with ownership of the house; the year was 1866. The owner of the house was named Anussi. At that point we had to end the seance.

We returned a few weeks later, and again Sybil Leek made contact with the

The ghost of a long-ago tenant in this Charles Street house keeps demanding justice. . . . and her property rights.

ghost. Picture my surprise when Elizabeth B. informed me that she had done some research on the house since our first meeting, and discovered that the house had indeed belonged to a family named Boyd ever since it had been bought by one Samuel Boyd in 1827! Even the landlord named "Anussi" turned out to have some basis of fact except that the name was spelled differently, Moeslin. According to the records, this man had rented the house to Mary Boyd in 1886. But what about the paper the ghost was trying to recover, the paper that apparently caused her continued presence in the house? "Find the paper, find the paper. This is my house," the ghost said, though the medium. The paper, it appeared, was in the name of her father, Bill, and the landlord did not have any right to the house according to the ghost. That was the reason for her continued presence there.

I tried to explain that much time had gone by, and that the matter was no longer of importance. I asked Miss Boyd to let go of the house and join her equally dead relatives on the other side of life. There was no doubt that medium Sybil Leek had indeed brought through an authentic ghost, because Elizabeth B. in discussing her research had mentioned only the name Mary Boyd. But in trance, the ghost speaking through the medium had identified herself proudly as Mary Elizabeth Boyd. When the records were rechecked it was discovered that the person living in the house in 1868 was Mary E. Boyd. There was also a William Boyd, evidently the father the ghost had referred to, who had given her the paper proving her ownership and rights to the house.

I do hope that no one will encounter Miss Mary Boyd again, for it would seem a pity that she has to hang around such a long time just to prove that the house was, after all, hers.

9
AARON BURR'S GHOST

 aron Burr, one-time vice-president of the United States, was a colorful political figure who is perhaps best remembered for the unhappy duel he fought with Alexander Hamilton at Weehawken, New Jersey, as a result of which Hamilton was killed. Even though the duel was a fair fight, and in terms of the early 19th century, a legitimate undertaking, Burr was accused of having murdered the brilliant young Hamilton and had to flee for his life eventually. Burr's political career was affected and in the end the Hamilton death prevented him from rising higher, perhaps becoming president of the United States. At a later date he led an expedition to the west to open up new territories. His political enemies accused him of sedition, of trying to start a new state in the west, and he was brought to trial. However, he was not found guilty of sedition. Nevertheless, this contributed to his further downfall and Aaron Burr died an embittered, unhappy man.

Down in Greenwich Village, New York's artistic district, on West 3rd Street on the corner of Sullivan Street there is a cafe which was known as the Cafe Bizarre, until some time ago; it now houses a restaurant. This is a very well preserved, three-story building dating back to pre-Revolutionary times and remodeled in the early 19th century. It is probably one of the oldest buildings in the area. At one time it formed part of Aaron Burr's stables, and prior to Burr's ownership, belonged to a British colonial family. The records show that Aaron Burr used it well into the 1830's, but how it was used later and after Burr's death is not clear.

The ground floor portion of the building is a kind of duplex loft, decorated with a bizarre motif even for a nightclub. The rear section of this room has been the center of ghostly manifestations. I have investigated the place on two occasions. A ghostly apparition of what may very well have been Aaron Burr, from the description, has appeared to a number of people working at the Cafe Bizarre. A waiter and the owner's wife, Mrs. Renee A. have described the intense-looking man in a white ruffled shirt with piercing black eyes and short beard. A visitor to the Cafe Bizarre, a young girl by the name of Alice M., also had a psychic experience in which she saw the same figure. As a result of my two investigations with mediums Ethel Johnson and later Sybil Leek, Mr. Burr's

Aaron Burr's stables, now a café,
where his restless spirit has been seen
by a number of people.

restless personality was freed from the place where so many emotional memories had kept him captive.

The trance interrogation was particularly dramatic. At first, the entity speaking through Mrs. Leek evaded my questions concerning its identity. At no time did "he" admit to being Aaron Burr. But under questioning, the spirit spoke of conditions only Burr would have been familiar with in these surroundings. For instance, at the very outset, the spirit cried out for Theo, asking me to find her for him. Theo had been Burr's only daughter, whom he had lost early in life. She was abroad a ship that never reached her destination and to this day we don't know whether the ship sank in a storm or fell victim to piracy.

Theo is a very unusual name. Only the Burr family had used it for its women during the period under investigation.

Another reason why I found the identity of the spirit convincing involved Burr's exile in France. Under questioning (and without prodding or leading questions on my part), the entity spoke of spending time in France. He spoke of wearing a beard and having to hide from his enemies. When I insisted that he tell me his name, he mentioned the name Arnot. Later research disclosed that Burr did have to hide from Napoleon's police, that he had a short beard when he returned from his French exile, and that the cover name he had used while in France was indeed Arnot. None of this could have been known to Mrs. Leek, or, for that matter, to me.

If you want to visit the place, remember that it is no longer the Cafe Bizarre but a different restaurant. The present owners may have no idea as to the background or history of the place. But you may still pick up the vibrations from the past though I doubt very much that Burr is still about.

10
THE HAUNTED TAVERN AT CLINTON, MARYLAND

 number of people have seen Abraham Lincoln's ghost walk the corridors of the White House, and others have reported unusual experiences at Ford's Theatre in Washington, where the actor John Wilkes Booth shot President Lincoln. Less known is an historical tavern in what it now Clinton, Maryland.

Thirteen miles south of Washington, in a small town now called Clinton but once known as Surrattville, stands an eighteenth-century building nowadays used as a museum. Mary Surratt ran it as an inn at the time when the area was far enough removed from Washington to serve as a way station to those travelling south from the nation's capital. When business fell off, however, Mrs. Surratt leased the eighteenth-century tavern to John Lloyd and moved to Washington where she ran a boardinghouse on H Street between Sixth and Seventh Streets. But she remained on close and friendly relations with her successor at the tavern at Surrattville, so that it was possible for her son John Surratt to use it as an occasional meeting place with his friends. These friends included John Wilkes Booth, and the meetings eventually led to the plot to assassinate President Lincoln.

After the murder, Booth escaped on horseback and made straight for the tavern. By prearrangement, he and an associate hid the guns they had with them in a cache in the floor of the tavern. Shortly after, he and the associate, David Herald, split up, and John Wilkes Booth continued his journey despite a broken foot. Eventually, he was discovered hiding at Garrett's barn and shot there.

The connection between Booth and the tavern was no longer public knowledge as the years went by. Some local people might have remembered it, but the outside world had lost interest. At one time the structure was acquired by John's brother the actor Edwin Booth, it appears. In the 1950's it passed into the

Mary Surratt's tavern was the place where Lincoln's murderers met and plotted: people have heard their voices here.

hands of a local businessman named Mr. M. By now the village was known as Clinton, since the Surrattville name had been changed shortly after the infamous trial of Mary Surratt.

The hauntings observed here include the figure of a woman, thought to be the restless spirit of Mary Surratt herself, whose home this had been at one time. Strange men have been observed sitting on the back stairs when there was no one about but the occupants of the house. Muffled voices of a group of men talking in excited tones have also been reported, and seem to indicate that at the very least an imprint from the past has been preserved at the Surratt Tavern. Many meetings of the conspirators had taken place in the downstairs part of the building, and when I brought Sybil Leek to the tavern she immediately pointed out the site of the meetings, the place where the guns had been hidden, and, in trance, established communication with the former owner of the tavern, Edwin Booth himself.

Although the building is now a museum and open to visitors, one should first obtain permission from Mr. M. at his supermarket, in Clinton, Maryland. Clinton itself is less than an hour's drive from downtown Washington. As far as I know there is no fee attached to a visit at Surratt Tavern. At the time when I made my investigation, Mr. M. had thought to sell the building to a museum or an historical trust, and by the time this appears in print, it may well have changed hands.

Anyone visiting the old tavern who is psychic might very well hear the same voices, or have some kind of psychic experience because the phenomena themselves have not faded away, nor are they likely to, since no formal exorcism has ever been attempted there.

11
THE DYING GASP

ne of the peculiarities of ghostly manifestations is that they repeat a certain traumatic happening over and over again as if they were phonograph records playing the same song without benefit of human hands. Whether these replays represent actual ghosts consciously reliving a terrible experience connected with their death or whether they are impressions left behind in the place where they occurred, is difficult to tell at times, although true ghostly manifestations are not always the same and one can distinguish certain differences and shadings in the way they occur to various witnesses. On the other hand, if we are dealing only with an imprint from the past which doesn't have any life of its own, the impression is likely to be exactly the same each time it is noticed.

Then of course there are atmospheric conditions, experiences clinging to the atmosphere of a house which do not necessarily represent anything of great dramatic shock value but may be the accumulation of past events in the house. Anyone who is sensitive, walking into such a place, will experience what is in the house in terms of accumulated "memories."

The case I am about to report on, however, does seem to have the earmarks of a true ghostly manifestation in that it represents an unresolved tragedy. Horace B. is a collector as well as an art expert. His house in Charlottesville, Virginia, is filled to the rafters with art and fine furniture. Carrsgrove, as the rambling country place is called, is a wooden structure, the oldest part of which dates back at least a hundred fifty years. Soon after acquiring the property, about 1956, the B.'s realized that there was something the matter with their house.

It was haunted. In the oldest part of the house, dead center, they kept hearing a "sighing" ghost.

Mrs. Helen B. had just given birth to a child when she first reported hearing the uncanny noise. At 3:45 A.M. every morning she heard the mournful sighing of

This Virginia mansion, privately owned, is the site of
a long-ago haunting, occasionally still heard upstairs.

a woman no one could see. At first only *she* heard it, but one day she woke her husband and insisted that he accompany her to the spot near the inner wall. Then he heard it, too.

Mr. B.'s curiosity was aroused and he made some inquiries about the house. The previous owner, whose name was McCue, had died, but his faithful nurse was still living. She reported what had happened one terrible morning in 1910.

McCue's daughter was staying at the house at the time with her young child. She started to imagine that the baby was not going to be normal, and in a fit of postnatal depression, she took poison. At exactly 3:45 A.M., the nurse told Mr. B., the father awoke and heard his daughter's *dying* gasp. By the time he raced to her bedroom on the other side of the house, she was dead.

It was that identical dying gasp that the B.'s had been hearing. However, once the explanation was given and the reasons for the noise in the house had been discussed, something happened to the ghost. The B.'s have not heard the noise lately.

The house is a private residence, but Mr. B. is a man possessed of true southern hospitality. He is the major force behind the local art museum and has been responsible for many of the cultural events taking place in Charlottesville, Virginia. Should you have the opportunity, I feel quite sure a visit to the home is within the possible.

12
THE GHOST ON FIFTH AVENUE

ifth Avenue, New York is generally thought of as a street of beautiful and expensive stores, the street where the St. Patrick's Day Parade takes place every March 17, and where people parade on Easter Sunday in their finery. But Fifth Avenue, especially the lower part of it, is very old New York; some of the houses still standing date back one hundred or even two hundred years.

Probably the most protracted investigation I have ever undertaken, and the most evidential case for the existence of ghosts, was the one that took me to 226 Fifth Avenue in New York City. I published the complete results in my first book, *Ghost Hunter,* after spending five months and seventeen separate sessions investigating this haunting.

226 Fifth Avenue was at one time an elegant town residence, later turned into an apartment house. At the time of my investigation in 1953, the top floor apartment, a duplex, belonged to a Captain Hassolt Davis, an explorer, who was abroad much of the time.

Seven years later, the apartment house was shut down for repairs. For about two or three years, it stood empty and began to look rather dismal. The area around the building is strictly commercial, and I thought it was only a matter of time before the building itself would be torn down to make room for a new skyscraper. Imagine my surprise when I recently passed the building. Far from being torn down, it has been reconditioned, and though it is no longer an elegant town house, and has commercial tenants on each floor, at least its basic structure has been maintained, the outside cleaned up, and the stairs still lead up to the top floor apartment that was once haunted.

Tenants of the top floor apartment prior to Captain Davis included Richard Harding Davis and the actor Richard Mansfield. We have no record of whether they were disturbed by the resident ghost or not, but Captain Davis was. Thanks to an introduction by the late *Daily News* columnist Danton Walker, I was able to enter the case in conjunction with a group of fellow students then working at the

Allegedly, the ghost of Confederate General Samuel Edward McGowen haunts this Fifth Avenue house, where he is said to have met foul play during the War Between the States.

headquarters of the Association for Research and Enlightenment. As a result of my long investigation, I learned of a Confederate hero officer crossing lines in the midst of war in order to see his trusty friend.

General Samuel Edward McGowan, of McGowan's Brigade, is historically documented to the fullest. There is of course no mention of his ghostly captivity at 226 Fifth Avenue, New York. To the official historian, he died later and lies buried in his hometown cemetery at Abbeyville, South Carolina. But the material coming through medium Ethel Johnson Meyers was so evidential and filled with detailed knowledge of the Civil War that I do not doubt in the least the harrowing account of McGowan's adventures in New York City.

Separation and war being what it was, the general's lady love, Mignon Guychone, of French Creole stock, had apparently taken up with another gentleman, named Walter, despite the fact that she loved the general and vice versa. Walter showed up unexpectedly and strangled General McGowan. In order not to be charged with murder, however, he made it appear like suicide, and hanged the lifeless body of the southern gentleman from the rafters in the little attic.

The most urgent need of the ghost—once he could communicate with us—was to set the record straight as to his suicide. Committing suicide was alien to the traditions of a gentleman officer, and McGowan was at great pains to explain that it was murder and not self-inflicted death.

There is now a coffee shop downstairs, but I doubt that those running the coffee shop know anything about the ghostly goings-on on the upper floors of the same house. Access to the upper floors may be difficult to a casual visitor, since this is a private house now. But if you are fortunate enough, perhaps you too may be able to visit the top floor where my investigation took place. At any rate, General Samuel Edward McGowan must by now be in much more pleasant surroundings as he has communicated with me from time to time. Those who hope to encounter his ghost may therefore not be able to do so, but the house still retains its Civil War charm and the *imprint* of past events certainly lingers on.

13
THE GAY STREET GHOST

I n the most picturesque part of Greenwich Village, New York's artists' quarters, there is a very old house which belonged to a famous puppeteer by the name of Frank Paris. The house at Number 12, Gay Street, contains a complete puppet theatre, a marvelous art collection, and a number of ghosts.

The house is a four-story building of the kind that was popular around the year 1800. It is in excellent condition and is one of the jewels of the area. Gay Street is just around the corner from bustling Sixth Avenue, and it is sometimes hard to find unless one knows how to get there.

Frank Paris turned the basement into a workshop for his puppet theatre. There, too, at various times he has given performances with his favorite puppets. The second story was turned into a duplex apartment for himself and his assistant. It is filled with old sculpture, antiques, paintings, and other witnesses of his vast and curious tastes. There are gargoyles, devils' masks, Javanese dancers, reflecting his fertile artistic talent.

The house remained unaltered until 1924, when a new section was added, covering a garden which used to exist in back of the house. At one time, Mayor Jimmie Walker owned this house and used it for one of his lady loves. Prior to Mr. Paris's ownership it belonged to real estate broker Mary Ellen Strunsky.

The owner, his friends, and even guests have experienced the sensation of unseen entities walking up and down the stairs at night, and on at least one occasion, a man in evening dress appeared at the door, smiling politely and then dissolving into thin air before the very eyes of reputable witnesses.

I first brought medium Betty Ritter to the house, and she made contact with a restless entity dating back to the prohibition era. She had no idea of the connection between Mayor Walker's "friend" and the house. Later Ethel Meyers brought through a French diplomat who complained he had been tortured here but had held on to his "secrets." There is evidence that the house did exist at the time of the Revolutionary War. Not long ago, medium Shawn Robbins came with me

The puppeteers' theatre was once next door to a morgue. Some of the "lost souls" from there have been observed in the theatre.

to the house for another visit, which was televised. Again, she made contact with a tortured soul who had died violently for holding on to "something." As for the gentleman in evening clothes, no one knows who he is.

Photographs taken of Frank Paris by a friend on one occasion showed a white something that was not visible to the naked eye. Paris had gradually gotten used to his unseen friends, and it did not disturb him in the least never to be quite alone. When one has a house of this antiquity standing in what must be one of the oldest streets in New York City, one naturally has to come to terms with the past. There are probably many unrecorded ghostly manifestations in other houses in the area, since much drama took place in this part of town during the early history of New York City. However, the people who have these houses are generally artistic and sophisticated individuals who don't mind having a ghost around, and who are not likely to complain about it.

14
JEAN HARLOW'S SPIRIT

he house where screen star Jean Harlow once lived had the reputation of being haunted by her, so I decided to investigate it. Today it belongs to a dentist and his wife and family, who are not particularly interested in pursuing the matter of psychic manifestations. It took the promise of anonymity for me to gain admittance, and so I must regretfully say, visitors are not encouraged.

The house in question is a handsome white stucco one-family house set back somewhat from a quiet residential street in Westwood, a section of Los Angeles near the University generally considered quiet and upper middle class. It is a two story building with an elegant staircase winding from the rear of the ground floor to the upper story. The downstairs portion contains a rather large, oblong living room which leads into a dining room. There are a kitchen and bathroom adjacent to that area and a stairway leading to the upper floor. Upstairs are two bedrooms and a bathroom.

When Dr. H., his wife and their two daughters moved into the house they did not realize that it had once belonged to Jean Harlow. I asked Mrs. H. what was the first thing she noticed after she had moved in.

"The day before we moved in I came over to direct the men who were laying the carpet," she replied, "I walked upstairs and my two dogs ran barking and growling into the upstairs bedroom. At that moment I thought I heard someone whisper in my ear and it scared me." But Mrs. H. looked around and she couldn't see anyone who could have whispered in her ear. "I could swear I heard somebody say, 'Please help me!' It was a soft whisper, sort of hushed. I talked to myself for a few minutes to get my bearings. I had never experienced anything of this kind. The night we moved in, my husband and I were lying in bed. Suddenly, it seemed as if the bed were hit by a very strong object three times. My husband said, 'My God, I'm getting out of here. This place is haunted.' I replied, 'Oh shush, it's all right if someone is trying to communicate. It's not going to hurt.' And to the ghost I said, 'You're welcome—how do you do; but we've got to get some sleep—we're very, very tired, so please let us be.' The bed never jerked after that again, but other things happened. There is a light switch on my oven in the kitchen. For a long time after we moved in the switch would go on every so often by itself.

One day at dusk I was walking from one room to another and coming through the dining room and for some reason I looked up at the ceiling. There was a light there which moved at the edges but it really didn't have any definite form. It looked more like a floating outline above me."

"Did anyone else experience anything unusual in the house?"

"On one occasion I was sitting right in the chair I'm in now and my Aunt Mary was in the other chair and we both heard sobs, terribly sad wrenching sobs, coming from the corner over there where the mailbox is. They were a woman's sobs. My aunt heard footsteps up and down the stairs when nobody was walking up or down and there are cold spots in various parts of the house. The footsteps, I feel, are a woman's because they are light. I've also felt things brush by my face touching my cheek. And I've smelled perfume in the upstairs children's

The living room at the house in Los Angeles that once belonged to Jean Harlow, whose presence is still being felt there.

bedroom—a very strong perfume. My little daughter who sleeps there doesn't have any perfume. Then there are strange drafts and cold winds all over the house, for no apparent reason."

The house was built in 1929. In the early 1930's Jean Harlow, on studio's orders, moved into it with her parents. She lived in it for four years. She married a man who was her agent but the marriage was not happy. Allegedly, the husband beat her and at one time she asked her parents to help her. Later, the husband committed suicide by shooting himself in the upstairs bedroom. This so upset her, Jean Harlow herself tried to commit suicide because she thought he killed himself over her. However, she did not die. It was then that Jean Harlow left this house and moved elsewhere. Most of the disturbances appeared to have taken place upstairs in and around the bedroom and bathroom.

The bedroom, once Jean Harlow's, where manifestations have occurred.

15
THE GHOST OF THE HEIRESS

Some of my readers may remember an old movie called "The Heiress," in which Olivia deHaviland fought against the iron will of her stern father who did not want her to marry a fortune hunter. Consequently, the heiress, as the girl was called, shut herself off from the world having been denied the man she loved, and died a recluse in her old mansion. The film itself was based on the well known novel, "Washington Square", by Henry James. James lived in the area and knew its history well indeed. The James novel is certainly based on fact, although he has embellished it with the freedom generally afforded novelists. The house, you see, didn't stand on Washington Square, New York City, but not too far away from it. It is called the Old Merchant's House, and currently is accessible to visitors as a local museum maintained privately but open to the public at certain hours. Surrounded by old houses, some of which are in a sad state of disrepair, the Old Merchant's House at 29 East 4th Street, Manhattan, stands out like a jewel in a generally low-class neighborhood, not far from the infamous Bowery where derelicts are still seen to this day, homeless men and women who make their precarious living by begging, and who have given the area a bad name in the past.

The house became the property of Seabury Tredwell, a wealthy merchant in the hardware business, as soon as it was completed by its builder. It was very convenient for his business.

The house is a Federal style building with windows opening onto Fourth Street. Originally a lovely garden surrounded the house, but today the garden is gone. The entrance is particularly imposing with two columns in classical style, at the top of a few steps and wrought-iron lanterns adorning the door. There are three floors topped by an attic, and there is also a basement.

Inside, the furniture is still of that period. There was a banister by Duncan Phyfe, and a fine staircase leading to the upper three stories. The downstairs was filled with fine furniture, some of it also by Duncan Phyfe, a rectangular piano

Immortalized by Henry James in the novel "Washington Square," the ghost of "the heiress" (played in the movie version by Olivia DeHavilland) has been seen in the Old Merchant's House.

which is still there, and in showcases along the walls one finds some of the costumes left behind.

The ghostly phenomena in the house center around Tredwell's three daughters, Phoebe, Sarah and Gertrude. According to tradition, Mr. Tredwell did not take kindly to any suitor who seemed to want to marry his daughters for their financial status.

The main manifestations occurred in the kitchen on the ground floor level in the rear of the house. But what used to be Gertrude's bedroom upstairs also has a presence in it from time to time. The ghost is that of a small elegant woman dressed in the finery of the middle nineteenth century. That this is Gertrude herself is very likely, since according to my psychic friend Ethel Johnson Meyers, it was she who died tragically here. There had been an unwanted baby, followed by disapproval of her actions by her family. That much of this can be proven objectively is doubtful, but a presence has been observed in the Old Merchant's House by several reliable witnesses, and no attempt has been made to exorcise her since after all this was her home.

One need not dwell upon the ghostly manifestations, as far as the curator is concerned, since she may not be aware of them. But I suggest a visit to the kitchen area, the back bedroom upstairs, and Gertrude's front bedroom. It contains a small canopied bed, which, according to at least one witness, is haunted.

One eerie story told about the Old Merchant's House concerns the fireplace on the third floor. Allegedly it cannot be photographed. I tried my luck with a very good camera while a professional photographer who was with me at the time also photographed the fireplace. Although the fireplace did not appear on both pictures, there is a strange white area around it that cannot be accounted for.

The Old Merchant's House merits a visit if only as an historical landmark and because of the well preserved costumes and utensils of a bygone era. There is a fascinating trapdoor on one of the upper floors, connected perhaps with secret rendezvous between Gertrude and her gentleman friend outside the house. At the time the house had a garden, and the river was not too far away. It was possible to approach the house on the East River, walk up the slanting acreage, which was then largely open, and visit the house. On the other hand, research has indicated that secret passageways existed between many of the houses in the area and the river, perhaps remnants of the revolutionary period when escape from dangers made such precautions advisable.

Gertrude's own clothes are still preserved in the showcases and nothing in the house has been changed from its original appearance. When the house was restored by a private committee of concerned citizens, great pain was taken to present everything the way it was when the house was at its best. Architect Joseph Roberto was in charge of these sensitive restorations, and it is largely to his credit that the Old Merchant's House today presents truly a major historical attraction, as well as the tantalizing prospect of meeting up with the dainty ghost of Gertrude Tredwell herself coming down the stairs to greet the visitor.

16

THE GHOSTS OF HELL'S KITCHEN, NEW YORK

ell's Kitchen is not an imaginary place in the devil's domain, but a somewhat rough and tough neighborhood in the heart of New York City. It is never advisable to walk there alone in the middle of night, but in the daytime it is as reasonably safe as any part of a large city these days. What makes the entire area even more fascinating is the fact that it is one of the most historically active areas of New York City, having been at one time, in revolutionary and colonial days, the uptown playground of the rich and important, such as the estate of Governor Clinton, whose house and gardens occupied a large area of what is now 44th Street through 46th Street, between Ninth and Eleventh Avenues.

Walking through the area today, one cannot be impressed by the beauty of the houses, for they are largely ordinary and frequently show their age without any grace. But a visitor to 420 West 46th Street, might be in for a great surprise if he manages to go through the narrow door that separates it from the street. This door leads to an open passage and a patio in back of the house. There he will find another house, connected to 420, marked 422-½ West 46th Street. This is Clinton Court, named after Governor George Clinton whose carriage house it once was. The ground itself was at one time used as a Potter's Field, the cemetery for the poor and the executed. Consequently, there are "presences" here in various spots, remainders from New York's past, when this area was fairly far "uptown."

When the British ruled New York, one of those buried here was a certain character known locally as "Old Moor," a sailor executed for mutiny.

His ghost was the first phantom seen at this place. In the 1820's, when the house was still used as a carriage house for the estate of Governor Clinton and his family, Old Moor would appear and frighten people. One day he frightened the wife of a coachman, who fell down the winding stairs to her death. These very stairs, leading from the upper story to the ground, still exist, although a second staircase, farther to the rear, has since disappeared. The coachman's wife became ghost number two.

The ghostly legend of the house was so well known that the Clinton children played a private game called "Ghosts." One day, one of the Clinton children, frightened by a real apparition, stumbled and fell to her death, becoming ghost number three. This child ghost was seen by the late Ruth Shaw, an artist who had rented the downstairs portion of the carriage house some years ago. All of the hauntings are confined to that part of the building. The front, giving onto 46th Street, has never been affected.

I have held several investigations at this address, including one with Ethel Johnson Meyers and another with Sybil Leek. I have also made a television film about it. Through Sybil, I met the ghost of a Colonial officer named Walker at 422-½ West 46th Street. Enough personal data was received and checked out in regimental records to prove that such a man existed and that, at any rate, the medium could not have known about it. He died in a duel.

Obviously there is a connection between this house and June Havock's town house, two blocks away. The ground on which both houses stand were both part of the same estate where Governor Clinton's mansion once stood. There may be other, undiscovered ghosts roaming the area, but the residents of the houses here are not likely to talk about them unless specifically asked. And it is not a wise thing to go around asking these people whether they have seen a ghost, because they are hard-working, generally poor people who need a ghost far less than they need proper employment.

While it is not difficult to walk into the courtyard of Clinton Court, as the house is still called, getting access to the two apartments is another matter. They are privately owned and do not look for visitors—especially not those who come for the ghosts rather than the flesh and blood people. Today the house is divided between two tenants. But since some of the phenomena have actually occurred outside the building, on the winding staircase and in the courtyard itself, it is entirely possible that a sensitive individual might experience *something* outside the apartments.

Governor Sir Henry Clinton's carriage house, now an elegant townhouse, is the site of a number of observed hauntings, a sailor, a coachman's wife and a child.

17

THE GHOST OF THE HESSIAN SOLDIER

ear Charlottesville, Virginia stands a farm house built during Revolutionary days, which was owned by a lady who we shall call Mary, who at one time worked with Professor Joseph B. Rhine at Duke University, and therefore had more than a passing interest in parapsychology. The house in question is a beautiful, well-kept, small manor house in the rolling country-side near Charlottesville, of the kind that made this part of the east truly outstanding historically. I came there in the company of writer Virginia Cloud, who is a very gifted amateur medium, and who had told the owner of the house about my interest in the ghostly goings-on. The oldest part of the house which is rather skillfully connected to the main house, consists of a hall, a main room and a small bedroom reached by a narrow winding staircase. This portion dates back to 1781 and has been the location of some very unusual happenings beginning with the time when Mary acquired the house and acreage around it in 1951. Whether earlier owners had any unusual experiences in the house I don't know, there was no way to talk to them. But at the time Mary moved in she was emotionally keyed up and perhaps this contributed to the experience that was to follow. She found herself in a small room downstairs which she had turned into a home bar, when she suddenly heard footsteps in the main room; the noise was that of someone wearing riding clothes, a sort of swishing sound. Naturally she called out to what she thought was a stranger, because she knew it could not be her husband who was away at the time. There was no answer and the steps continued; someone was walking up and down in the room. Mary looked out the window and outside near the barn she saw the rest of her family unaware of what was transpiring inside the house. This upset her even more, so she decided to step into the main room herself. There was no one

A Hessian soldier died in this, his last refuge, unable to leave to this day.

in there, but even though she could not see anyone she heard the steps continue in her presence, until they reached the doorway, and then they went back across the room to the stairway where they stopped abruptly at the landing leading to the old room above it. It was at this moment that Mary recalled a conversation with the previous owner. It appears that a certain Mrs. Erly who had lived in the house before, had heard a strange noise, as if someone were falling down those stairs, yet she could not see anyone.

Two years later, in 1953, her two daughters who were then aged twelve and nine, happened to be playing in the upstairs room while the parents were entertaining guests in the smaller portion of the house connected to the main house by a covered walk. The time was about 10:00 P.M. when they distinctly heard someone walk around downstairs in what they knew was an empty house. They called out but received no reply. At first they thought it might have been a friend of their parents but on checking later discovered that nobody had left the party to return to the main house even for a moment.

Several years later Mary again heard the by-now-familiar footsteps in the same area of the house. They would start, then stop again, then start up again.

Mary decided to investigate the background of her old house. She discovered that there were three family cemeteries on the grounds and that the house itself went back to 1781. Prior to her owning the house, the fireplace had been rebuilt and at that time an inscription was found explaining that a Hessian soldier-prisoner from a nearby barrack had helped build that particular chimney in 1781. Mary then discovered that three thousand prisoners of war had been kept in barracks nearby, mainly Hessian soldiers who had come to America against their wishes, serving with the British. Some of these Hessian soldiers had stayed on after the Revolutionary War and married local girls.

None of this was discussed with Virginia Cloud who entered the house and went into a semi-trance state. She described a soldier named Alfred or Albert, wearing white shirt, boots and trousers and dragging himself into the house apparently with a foot injury. Just as Virginia was reliving the soldier's tale of horror, all of us heard a faint knock at the entrance door, and when we went to open it there was no one there. There is no doubt in my mind that the Hessian soldier deserter who wanted to find a last refuge from the pursuing Redcoats died in that house and somehow did not realize that he was no longer in the physical body.

The house is in private hands and I doubt that it can be visited.

18
THE HOLLYWOOD PARTY GHOST

rden Boulevard is in a highly respectable and rather attractive section of Hollywood and contains mainly attractive, small houses with gardens behind them. Back in 1963 I was a panelist on a television program and shortly afterwards received a letter from a lady who seemed to be very upset about the ghosts in her house. As soon as I could, I paid her a visit. She seemed calmer now as she explained what had happened in the house.

"My mother bought our home around thirty-eight years ago. It had just been completed when we moved in. Unfortunately, two years later financial reverses forced us to rent the house out to strangers and live elsewhere. There were five different tenants during a nine-year period when we did not live at the house. But during that time my mother received a call from our former next-door neighbors telling her that the people who were living in our house had had a party, as a result of which a terrible fight had occurred and that they could hear furniture being broken and almost had called the police. When the last tenants moved out my mother discovered that it was all too true, furniture had indeed been broken. We moved back in and tried to settle down in what was again our house. There are two bedrooms in back of the house and a small room which we use as a den. These three rooms have French doors and open into a good sized patio or garden.

"A short time after we had returned to our house strange things began to happen. I was then about twenty years old. One night when everyone had gone to bed and my sister had gone out, and I was writing a letter in my bedroom, my locked French doors started to rattle and shake as if someone was desperately trying to get in. It so happens that we had just painted the patio floor and that the paint was still wet. The next morning I looked outside for any footprints but there

*A young girl died during a wild party
at this Hollywood house. Her ghost
was seen, and the revellers heard,
only a few years ago.*

were none. Whoever it was who had rattled our door certainly didn't leave any footprints. Next we would hear a light switch being turned now and then when there was no one in the room. During that period I was married and one night, when my husband was outside the house, I was alone. This was around 9:00 P.M., when I suddenly heard someone turning the knob of the door leading from the laundry to the den. I looked and I actually saw the knob being turned by unseen hands! When my husband returned later we looked all over the house but there was no intruder. Every window was bolted, every door was locked. Later I divorced my husband and kept company with another man. One night we returned to the house, which was then empty, when we both clearly heard footsteps coming toward the door from inside the house, as if to meet us."

The phenomenon kept continuing, and Helen, her aged mother and her sister all experienced it. Once Helen found herself at an unseen party, hearing a champagne cork popping and liquid being poured right beside her, yet she could see nothing. This experience repeated itself from time to time in six week intervals. The party apparently took place in what was then her bedroom. Someone kept whistling songs inside the house when they could not see anyone. Objects on the dressing table would move by their own volition while everyone was in bed at night. In the middle of the night, Helen would hear someone in the kitchen, kettles being handled, cupboards being opened, as if there was someone looking for something—yet when she checked she found there was no one in the kitchen. But the worst came about three years prior to her getting in touch with me.

"One night about three years ago," she explained, "I got up around midnight to go to the bathroom. While I was in the bathroom I heard loudly and clearly a terrible fight going on in the living room. It was a wordless and desperate struggle. How I got the courage to open the door to the living room I'll never know, but I did. It was completely dark. I saw nothing and the fighting stopped the instant I opened the door!"

Hardly had they recovered from this experience when Helen, her mother and her sister became witnesses to another fight scene right outside their bedrooms on the patio. It sounded as if every stick of their patio furniture was being broken by people who were fighting desperately but wordlessly, and it lasted several minutes. Needless to say that when they checked the next morning, none of their furniture had been touched. Everything was in its place and looked as pretty as it had always been.

There is a double garage on the premises and whenever Helen and her family had guests, she and her mother would sleep in the garage. Whenever they did so, they would be awakened at night by heavy footsteps walking up to the garage door. They never heard anyone walking away from the garage, however. Since the entire property is enclosed by very high fences and a steel gate across the driveway, it is practically impossible for a human intruder to get into the house or patio. One night Helen had dozed off while watching television when she was rudely awakened by a voice enunciating very clearly and saying loudly, "Oh woe, woe, you've got to go, go, go!"

But Helen had no intention of giving up the house she loved so much. Instead, she got in touch with me. I came to the house the following April in the company of a medium gifted with photography mediumship as well as clairvoyance. The lady's name was Maxine Bell, and she had come highly recommended by the American Society for Psychical Research in Los Angeles. While Mrs. Bell sat in the front living room I entered the bedroom, which had been the center of most of the activities by the ghost. There I set up my Zeiss camera, and took a number of black and white photographs with time exposure. One of the pictures, when developed under test conditions, clearly shows the figure of a very young girl in a flimsy dress standing near the window of the bedroom. Since there had been no one in the room but I, and as the camera was in perfect condition and the development and printing had been done by a laboratory, there was no reason to suspect any foul play. What I came to call the "Ghost in a negligee" turned out to be the surviving spirit of a very young girl who had apparently fallen victim to that terrible fight Helen and her family kept hearing in the dark. It appeared that a young girl's body might still be buried in the garden and that her appearance and the subsequent disturbances were connected with it. But no matter how I pleaded with Helen to have the garden dug up to look for the body, she refused out of fear that the neighbors might have strange ideas about it. I haven't heard much from Helen lately and so I am not sure whether the young spirit is still about or whether the wild party is still going on night after night in Helen's bedroom.

19
THE GHOST OF HUNGRY LUCY

he well-known stage and screen actress June Havoc owned a town house in New York City until recently which stood in a very old part of town. Located on West 44th Street, near Ninth Avenue, Manhattan, this impressive Victorian town house was built over a hundred years ago and was originally the property of the Rodenberg family. It has four stories and at the time when it was built, was considered one of the most elegant houses in the area. Today the area is known as Hell's Kitchen and considered less than desirable as a neighborhood. Eventually the house fell into disrepair but was restored to its original appearance both inside and outside by an architect in the 1950's. June Havoc acquired it in 1962 and rented the upper floors to various tenants but kept the downstairs apartment for herself. One reaches Miss Havoc's apartment by a staircase up to the parlor floor. For some unknown reason, tenants never stayed very long in that apartment but Miss Havoc paid no attention at the time she moved in. Before long, however, she noticed a number of things. There were strange tapping noises at various times of day and night and eventually they kept her from sleeping or concentrating on her work. This became particularly loud around 3:00 in the morning. At first she tried to find a logical explanation for the noises by calling in all sorts of workmen and experts to see whether the house was settling or whether there was something wrong with the piping or the structure of the house. None of these things turned out to be true. When the noises became unbearable Miss Havoc called upon me to help her rid the house of whatever was causing the disturbances. I paid the house two visits in the company of famed British medium Sybil Leek. On the first occasion we had the company of several distinguished observers, including newspaper columnist Earl Wilson and publicist Gail Benedict. As soon as Sybil Leek had slipped into a trance state during which her own personality was temporary absent while the alleged ghost was invited to speak through her, it

became apparent that something very dramatic had taken place in the house.

A young woman ghost calling herself Lucy manifested through the medium, crying out in pain of hunger and demanding food. During my questioning it appeared that "Hungry Lucy," as I later came to call her, had lived and died on the spot where the house now stands. Her death had been, according to her own testimony, due to a fever epidemic. She claimed to have lived in the year 1792. I then demanded to know why Lucy was still in the house, what she was looking for. She explained she was waiting for her boyfriend, a soldier by the name of

"Hungry Lucy," the ghost of a camp follower from Colonial days, has been creating havoc in what used to be actress June Havoc's townhouse.

Alfred. Since it is possible to check into the regiments of soldiers even several hundred years ago I asked what regiment did her Alfred serve in. Without hesitation Lucy replied, "Napier." The following day we checked this out and discovered that Colonel Napier was the commanding officer of a regiment stationed in the grounds of Governor Clinton's estate. The land on which Miss Havoc's house stands was part of that estate in 1792. Further, we found that a fever epidemic had in fact occurred at that time and Colonel Napier himself had been shipped back to England because of illness. During the seance we convinced Lucy that there was no point in waiting around for her soldier any longer, and eventually she let go of her compulsion to stay on in the house. Soon she was slipping away and I left Miss Havoc's apartment in the hope that all would be quiet from then on.

However, this was not the case. It appears that while we had freed Lucy from the house, we had done nothing about Alfred, her boyfriend who had also died in the area. A second visit was arranged during which Sybil Leek went into deep trance again. This time additional contacts were made with men who had lived and died in the area during the Revolutionary period and we were able to establish that these people had actually existed from comparing their names with entries in regimental and other historical records. We also addressed ourselves to Alfred imploring him to let go since his Lucy was now "on the other side of life," that is to say no longer among the living. We should have done this at the same time we dispatched Lucy to her just rewards. Unfortunately, Alfred failed to understand us and though the seance was otherwise successful, the noises continued sporadically. In 1969 June Havoc sold the house and with it relinquished her tenancy of the downstairs apartment. But I hear from people living in the house, now and again, that Alfred is still about.

A séance held at the house with the late Sybil Leek as medium.

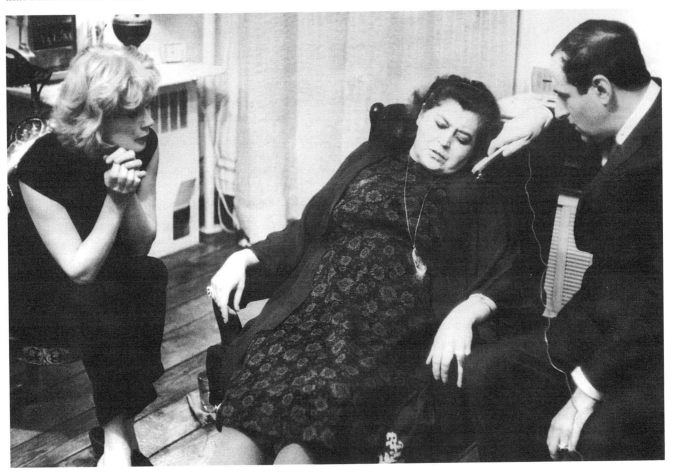

20
THE INTEGRATION GHOST

n the early 1960s when black people and white people were still looking at each other with a sense of bewilderment instead of accepting each other as people whom God had made different by color, but who shared a common humanity, there lived a certain John Gray, whose profession was in the advertising business. Mr. Gray was well-liked by his colleagues and superiors, and was what one would today call a success as an account executive, a man of whom the agency for whom he worked was justly proud. In the world of Madison Avenue, white people filled all the desirable jobs in agencies in those years, and Mr. Gray had no intention of revealing the one secret he took with him to his death: that he was a black man, with very light skin who had decided to "pass" as a white man in a white man's world. He died of cancer after a long illness and it was only when his family provided him with a real old-fashioned southern funeral that it became clear what his ethnic background was. I'm sure that John Gray himself would have been appalled at the way he was being laid to rest as he had preferred to be cremated, and have his ashes spread over those parts of Manhattan where he would not have been allowed to live had he been known as a black man in those days.

Let me backtrack a little. The year is 1961. Bob and Frank share an apartment in the Grand Central area of New York City. Both of them work in the advertising and promotional field, but Frank is white and Bob is black. Bob then had a friend, the aforementioned John Gray, who at age 33 knew he had a terminal illness. Because of his illness he was no longer working in the advertising field but had taken a city job with odd working hours which usually brought him home to his apartment at 34th Street and Third Avenue in the middle of the afternoon. Three months after Gray's death the two friends, Frank and Bob, decided to take over what was once John's apartment. It wasn't long after they had moved in and Frank was alone in the apartment, resting in bed, reading a book when he clearly heard the front door open and close, as if by itself. This was followed by a man's footsteps which he could clearly hear resound on the bare floor. "Who is it?" Frank called out wondering who could come up to his place in the middle of the afternoon. But no one answered, and the footsteps continued slowly to the bedroom door which lies to the right of the large living room area of the small apartment several flights up. Now Frank heard the characteristic noise of the bedroom door opening and then closing and the footsteps continuing on into the room toward his bed. There they stopped abruptly. Frank was naturally terrified for he couldn't see anything in the way of a human being to whom the footsteps could belong. Since this happened at 3:00 in the afternoon in good daylight, he was naturally upset. There was a moment of total silence. Then the unseen visitor's footsteps seemed to turn around and he was slowly walking out again, the noise of the door opening and closing was repeated in the same way and yet the door did not actually open.

Frank thought about it for an hour or two, then decided it might have been his

A black gentleman who passed as white years ago, lived and died in this old house . . . but never left.

imagination. He felt he should not share the odd experience with his apartment mate, Bob, and nothing more happened to bring it back to his mind until about six weeks later. It was then that Bob had an identical experience; alone in bed he heard the footsteps, he heard the door open and close but it did not seem to panic him. Bob, apparently, was more psychic than Frank: his innate psychic sense told him that it was his departed friend John Gray paying his former apartment a visit! Without thinking twice Bob leaned forward in bed and said in a low but clear voice toward the unseen visitor, "May your soul rest in peace John." When he had said this, the unseen feet moved on and the footsteps went out the way they had come in. It was then that the two friends discussed their psychic experiences and realized that they had heard precisely the same phenomenon. Eventually they changed apartments again and the little place on Third Avenue near 34th Street was soon forgotten. Three years later Frank found himself at a social gathering in the same area when he overheard one of the guests talk about a friend by the name of Vernon who had just moved out of a "haunted apartment" because he couldn't stand it any longer. Suddenly Frank realized they were talking about the same apartment. For a while the place remained unoccupied, then the building passed into the hands of a fish restaurant which still owns it. Most of the tenants in this five story walk-up are either artists or business people. The building is well kept and the apartments are all quite small.

I decided to follow up the story. Upon visiting the haunted apartment, second building on the northeast side of Third Avenue from 34th Street on uptown, I met the then occupants, a film editor and his wife. Both of them had had some experiences in the apartment also but had so far not decided to move out.

On July 22, 1964 I came to the apartment with medium Ethel Johnson Meyers to try and make contact with what appeared to be a still restless ghost. As soon as she was in deep trance, the medium described the "dark complexed" man, who was looking rather intently at Frank and his former apartment mate Bob who had come along to the seance. In the trance state John Gray took over the body of the medium, speaking in a very emotional and deep masculine voice to his erstwhile friends. At first he could not understand that they would not recognize him, complaining bitterly that they had failed to visit him lately. Gently I explained that he had passed over to the next stage of existence but John refused to accept this, thinking that we were all mad to suggest such a thing. As with most ghosts he did not realize that he himself was what is commonly called dead. Gradually he understood, but this did not help his suffering. Where was he to go? "This is my house" he kept repeating over and over. Finally, we persuaded the restless one to let go and as the medium returned to her own body and faculties, John Gray slipped away. I sincerely hope he has found peace on the other side of life, and if any of my readers chance to visit the house on Third Avenue and still feel him about, would they please say a kindly word to him so that he may find whatever remains to be found to give him full and everlasting peace of mind.

21 JEFFERSON'S SPIRIT AND MONTICELLO

here's hardly any need to explain who Thomas Jefferson was, but perhaps there should be some light shed on the curious interest of our present day historians concerning Jefferson. Much new material about his private life has lately come to light, and the architect of the Declaration of Independence does seem to have had his more human side as well as his patriotic image.

Monticello, which every schoolboy knows from its representation on the American five-cent piece, is probably one of the finest examples of American architecture, designed by Jefferson himself, who lies buried here in the family graveyard. It stands on a hill looking down into the valley of Charlottesville, perhaps fifteen minutes from the town proper. Carefully landscaped grounds surround the house. Inside, the house is laid out in classical proportions. From the entrance hall with its famous clock, also designed by Jefferson, one enters a large, round room, the heart of the house. On both sides of this central area are rectangular rooms. To the left is a corner room, used as a study and library from where Jefferson, frequently early in the morning before anyone else was up, used to look out on the rolling hills of Virginia. Adjacent to it is a very small bedroom, almost a bunk. Thus, the entire west wing of the building is a self-contained apartment in which Jefferson could be active without interfering with the rest of his family. On the other side of the round central room is a large dining room leading to a terrace which, in turn, continues into an open walk with a magnificent view of the hillside. The furniture is Jefferson's own, as are the silver and china, some of it returned to Monticello in recent years by history-conscious citizens of the area who had purchased it in various ways.

But it was the little honeymoon cottage behind the main house that attracted my psychic friend Ingrid more than other rooms in the main house. Built in the same classical American style as Monticello itself, the building contained two fair-sized rooms, on two stories. A walk led to the entrance to the upper story, barricaded by an iron grillwork to keep the tourists out. After a while I turned to my psychic friend, Ingrid Beckman, asking her what impressions she received from the honeymoon cottage.

"Well, I think the wife was not living on her level, her standard, and she was unhappy. It wasn't what she was used to. It wasn't grand enough. I think she had doubts about him and his plans."

"In what sense?"

"I think she was dubious about what would happen. She was worried that he was getting too involved, and she didn't like his political affiliations too well."

I turned to Horace for comments. To my surprise, Horace asked me to turn off my tape recorder since the information was of a highly confidential nature. However, he pointed out that the material could be found in *American Heritage,* and that I was free to tell the story in my own words.

Apparently, there had always been a problem between Jefferson and his wife concerning other women. His associations were many and varied. All this did not contribute to Mrs. Jefferson's happiness. Gossip and legend intermingle in small towns and in the countryside. This is especially true when important historical figures are involved.

Could it be that part of Thomas Jefferson still clings to this little cottage where he found much happiness? A visit with Mr. Jefferson, one way or another, should prove rewarding if only for historical reasons. But then one never knows, if the visitor is psychic, what might happen.

Thomas Jefferson's psychic imprint is still to be felt at the house he designed, built, and lived in.

22

MADAME JUMEL'S GHOST

ou wouldn't think that in the bustling city of New York, right in the heart of Manhattan, there stands a magnificent southern styled mansion with several ghosts in it. But the fact of the matter is that there is such a building, nowadays known as the Morris-Jumel mansion in Washington Heights, Manhattan, at the corner of 160th Street and Edgecombe Avenue. I've been to this mansion several times, twice as part of an investigation into the hauntings reported and several times more with friends, some of whom felt chilly and disturbed by the continuing presences in the building.

Built at the highest spot of Manhattan originally called Harlem Heights, the mansion was erected by the British born Colonel Roger Morris and in 1776, during the Revolutionary War, General George Washington made it his headquarters during the battle of Long Island. Later on, when the fortunes of war changed, the British moved in again, and General Sir Henry Clinton stayed at the mansion. From then on in the career of this magnificent building was somewhat checkered. At one point it served as an ordinary tavern called Calumet Hall. One day in 1810, a French wine merchant, recently arrived on these shores, by the name of Stephen Jumel, and his ambitious American-born wife passed by and decided to buy the place on the spot. At that time the property included thirty-five acres of land surrounding it. Madame Jumel immediately refurbished and renovated the place and it soon became one of the show places of New York City.

There are four stories and a basement and the principal areas of psychic activity are the second and third floors as well as the balcony which can be seen from a distance away. It was on that balcony on January 19, 1964 that a small group of school children saw the ghost of Madame Jumel. It all happened when they were waiting to be let into the historical building. They had arrived a little early, and were becoming restless, when one of the children pointed to the balcony where a lady in a flimsy violet-colored gown had just appeared. "Shush!" she said to the children, trying to calm them down. After that she simply receded into the room behind the balcony. It never occurred to the children until later that she had never opened the doors but had simply vanished through the closed doors. When the curator, Mrs. C., arrived to let them in, they complained that they could have been in the house much sooner and why didn't the lady on the balcony open up for them? Needless to say there was no lady on the balcony as far as the curator was concerned. But she soon realized that she was presiding over a much haunted house.

One flight up in what used to be Madame Jumel's own bedroom I held a seance with the help of Ethel Johnson Meyers, during which the late Stephen Jumel complained bitterly about being murdered by his own wife. He had fallen off a haywagon and hurt himself on a pitchfork, and a doctor had been summoned to

The Morris-Jumel Mansion in Washington Heights, New York, has a ghostly couple to this day: Stephen Jumel, the French wine merchant, and his wife, Betsy Jumel, responsible for his death.

attend to his wounds. As soon as the doctor had left, however, Mrs. Jumel tore off the bandages and Stephen bled to death. I tried to have his tomb reopened in a nearby cemetery but never received official permission to do so. The one-time Vice President of the United States, Aaron Burr, famous political figure of the first half of the nineteenth century, was even then friendly with the later Widow Jumel. He, in fact, married her and spent much time at the mansion. His presence has also been felt by many visitors. As if having an angry victim of foul play in the house and perhaps the lingering spirit of Madame Jumel herself were not enough, there is also a young servant girl who became involved with one of the family and committed suicide by jumping out the window. She may be one of the ghosts observed on the top floor where the servants' quarters were located. Since I conducted two "rescue" seances at the mansion during which Stephen Jumel had the opportunity to complain about his untimely death, I feel that he has been pacified and is no longer a resident of the Morris-Jumel mansion. But Madame Jumel herself and the servant girl may well still roam the corridors of the house where they once lived, the one in unusual splendor, the other in great anguish.

Not long ago a school teacher brought his class from a nearby school to visit the famed mansion. While the children were inspecting the lower two floors he dashed up to the top floor, being a history buff, most eager to inspect the house from top to bottom. Picture his surprise when he was confronted by a Revolutionary soldier who had practically stepped out of a painting on the top floor! The teacher fainted on the spot and was revived later.

Not so lucky was another visitor, again a teacher, who, having a history of heart disease, was frightened to death on one of the floors. But this is unusual: ghosts do not hurt people, ghosts should not frighten people because they are, after all, only human beings in trouble *with themselves*.

The Morris-Jumel mansion can be visited every day until 4:00 P.M. It is maintained now as a museum and there is no special reservation necessary to visit. However, certain rooms of the upper floors have been closed off to the public now, whether for reasons of expediency or because of the continuing strong interests in ghosts is hard to say. The personnel serving in the mansion knows nothing about the ghostly manifestations, so there is no point in questioning them about it.

23

THE GHOST
OF THE LITTLE
WHITE FLOWER

rs. D. and her son Bucky lived in a comfortable house on a hilltop in suburban Kentucky, not far from Cincinnati, Ohio, a pleasant, white house, not much different from other houses in the area. The surroundings are lovely and peaceful, and there's a little man-made pond right in front of the house. Nothing about the house or the area looks the least bit ghostly or unusual. Nevertheless Mrs. D. needed my help in a very vexing situation.

Six months after Mrs. D. had moved into the house, she began to hear footsteps upstairs when there was no one about, and the sound of a marble being rolled across the hall. Anything supernatural was totally alien to Mrs. D.

Nevertheless, Mrs. D. had a questioning and alert mind, and was not about to accept these phenomena without finding out what caused them. When the manifestations persisted, she walked up to the foot of the stairs and yelled, "Why don't you just come out and show yourself or say something instead of making all those noises?"

As if in answer, an upstairs door slammed shut and then there was utter silence. After a moment's hesitation, Mrs. D. dashed upstairs and made a complete search. There was no one about and the marble, which seemingly had rolled across the floor, was nowhere to be seen.

When the second Christmas in the new house rolled around, the D.'s were expecting Bucky home from the army. He was going to bring his sergeant and the sergeant's wife with him, since they had become very friendly. They celebrated New Year's Eve in style and high spirits (not the ethereal kind, but the bottled type). Nevertheless, they were far from inebriated when the sergeant suggested that New Year's Eve was a particularly suitable night for a seance. Mrs. D. would have no part of it at first. She had read all about phony seances and such, and remembered what her Bible said about such matters. Her husband had long gone to bed. The four of them decided to have a go at it. They joined hands and sat quietly in front of the fireplace. Nothing much happened for a while. Then

Bucky, who had read some books on psychic phenomena, suggested that they needed a guide or control from the other side of life to help them, but no one had any suggestions concerning to whom they might turn. More in jest than as a serious proposal, Mrs. D. heard herself say, "Why don't you call your Indian ancestor, Little White Flower!" Mr. D. is part Cherokee, and Bucky, the son, would, of course, consider this part of his inheritance too. Mrs. D. protested that all this was nonsense, and that they should go to bed. She assured them that nothing was likely to happen. But the other three were too busy to reply, staring behind her into the fireplace. When she followed the direction of their eyes she saw what appeared to be some kind of light similar to that made by a flashlight. It stayed on for a short time and then disappeared altogether.

From that day on Mrs. D. started to find strange objects around the house that had not been there a moment before. They were little stones in the shape of Indian arrows. She threw them out as fast as she found them. Several weeks later, when she was changing the sheets on her bed, she noticed a huge red arrow had been painted on the bottom sheet—by unseen hands.

It was in the winter of 1963. One afternoon she was lying down on the couch with a book trying to rest. Before long she was asleep. Suddenly she awoke with a feeling of horror which seemed to start at her feet and gradually work its way up throughout her entire body and mind. The room seemed to be permeated with something terribly evil. She could neither see nor hear anything, but she had the

The ghost of "little White Flower," an Indian girl, has kept people in this Kentucky residence on their toes. The ghost materialized in front of this fireplace.

feeling that there was a presence there and that it was very strong and about to overcome her.

For a few weeks she felt quite alone in the house, but then things started up again. The little stone arrowheads appeared out of nowhere again all over the house. Hysterical with fear, Mrs. D. called upon a friend who had dabbled in metaphysics and asked for advice. The friend advised a seance in order to ask Little White Flower to leave.

Although Little White Flower was not in evidence continuously and seemed to come and go, Mrs. D. felt the Indian woman's influence upon her at all times. Later the same week, Little White Flower put in another appearance, this time visual. It was toward four o'clock in the morning, when Mrs. D. woke up with the firm impression that her tormentor was in the room. As she looked out into the hall, she saw on the wall a little red object resembling a human eye, and directly below it what seemed like half a mouth. Looking closer, she discerned two red eyes and a white mouth below. It reminded her of some clowns she had seen in the circus. The vision remained on the wall for two or three minutes, and then vanished completely.

After several postponements I was finally able to come to Kentucky and meet with Mrs. D. in person. On June 20, 1964, I sat opposite the slightly portly, middle-aged lady who had corresponded with me for several months so voluminously.

As I intoned my solemn exorcism and demanded Little White Flower's withdrawal from the spot, I could hear Mrs. D. crying hysterically. It was almost as if some part of her was being torn out and for a while it seemed that *she* was being sent away, not Little White Flower.

The house has been quiet ever since; Little White Flower has presumably gone back to her own people and Mrs. D. continues living in the house without further disturbances.

24
A VISIT WITH CAROLE LOMBARD'S GHOST

In 1967 I first heard of a haunted house where the late Carole Lombard had lived. Adriana S. was by vocation a poet and writer, but she made her living in various ways, usually as a housekeeper. In the late forties she had been engaged as such by a motion picture producer of some renown. She supervised the staff, a job she performed very well indeed, being an excellent organizer. Carefully inspecting the house before agreeing to take the position, she had found it one of those quiet elegant houses in the best part of Hollywood that could harbor nothing but good. Confidently, Adriana took the job.

A day or two after her arrival, when she was fast asleep in her room, she found herself aroused in the middle of the night by someone shaking her. Fully awake, she realized that she was being shaken by the shoulder. She sat up in bed, but there was no one to be seen. Even though she could not with her ordinary sight distinguish any human being in the room, her psychic sense told her immediately that there was someone standing next to her bed. Relaxing for a moment and closing her eyes, Adriana tried to tune in on the unseen entity. Immediately she saw, standing next to her bed, a tall, slim woman with blonde hair down to her shoulders. What made the apparition or psychic impression the more upsetting to Adriana was the fact that the woman was bathed in blood and quite obviously suffering.

Adriana realized that she had been contacted by a ghostly entity but could not get herself to accept the reality of the phenomenon, and hopefully ascribed it to an upset stomach, or to the new surroundings and the strains of having just moved in. At the same time, she prayed for the restless one. But six or seven days later the same thing happened again. This time Adriana was able to see the ghost more clearly. She was impressed with the great beauty of the woman she saw and decided to talk about her experience with her employers in the morning. The producer's wife listened very quietly to the description of the ghostly visitor, then nodded. When Adriana mentioned that the apparition had been wearing a light suit covered with blood, the lady of the house drew back in surprise. It was only then that Adriana learned that the house had once been Carole Lombard's and that the late movie star had lived in it very happily with Clark Gable. Carole Lombard had died tragically in an airplane accident during World War II, when her plane, en route to the East where she was going to do some USO shows, hit a mountain during a storm. At the time, she was wearing a light colored suit.

Several years afterwards I investigated the house in the company of an actress who is very psychic. It so happened that the house now belonged to her doctor, a lady by the name of Doris A. In trance, my actress friend was able to make contact with the spirit of Carole Lombard. What kept her coming back to the house where she once lived was a feeling of regret for having left Clark Gable, and also the fact that she and Gable had had a quarrel just before her death. Luckily, we were able to pacify the restless spirit, and presumably the house is now peaceful.

25

MARY AND THE PIRATE

I n one of the most beautiful parts of New Hampshire, there is a truly impressive New England mansion known nowadays as the Ocean-born Mary House, a name which has stuck to it ever since it was built by a certain Mary Wallace who was born aboard ship while crossing over to the New World. I have been to the Ocean-born Mary House several times and conducted three separate investigations there with two different mediums, and the material was truly astounding. So were the eyewitness accounts of those who have seen a ghost in the house or at the window.

Nevertheless, because neighborhood youths kept making the house a target for their Halloween pranks, the owners began to shy away from the true story and eventually told eager tourists that there was nothing to the ghosts after all and to please not bother them.

Mary was the ocean-born child who was befriended by a pirate, named Don Pedro. Later in life he helped her build this house and in turn she permitted him to spend his old age as her pensioner. Unfortunately for Don Pedro, so the story goes, one of his men who had been disgruntled, caught up with him, and in the ensuing fight Don Pedro was killed. Allegedly his body lies underneath the fireplace, but there is no proof since the fireplace has never been dug up.

The place came to my attention when a local amateur medium, Mrs. A., asked my assistance in dealing with the phenomena she had encountered at the house. During a routine visit as a tourist, she had found herself practically taken over by the spirit of Mary Wallace who demanded to be heard through her. Frightened, she fled the home to a Boston suburb. That night she awoke and, without being able to resist, drove her car all the way up to New Hampshire, still in her nightclothes.

I brought Mrs. A. back to Ocean-born Mary's with me, in the daytime and

The stately "Ocean-born Mary house"
in New Hampshire, built by a pirate,
boasts the spirit of Mary Wallace, still
protecting it.

wearing street clothes, and in trance Mary Wallace manifested. The gist of her communication through the medium was a concern for the proper maintenance of the old house and an almost playful desire to be acknowledged and recognized.

Subsequent to this visit I also drove up with Sybil Leek and attempted another trance session. Sybil managed to bring through a servant girl who had apparently met with foul play or was involved in it. At any rate, she must be the third resident ghost, in addition to Mary Wallace and her pirate friend.

There was also talk of a buried treasure somewhere on the grounds. The directions were quite explicit and after Sybil came out of trance, we all went out and looked for the treasure underneath the stones behind the house. We did not dig, of course, and treasures have a way of staying underground, especially after two hundred and fifty years.

While there may be more speculation about the reality of the hidden treasure and possibly of the continued residence "in spirit" of the pirate, there is substantial evidence that the house is haunted by a woman greatly resembling the original owner.

A number of people have seen the tall, stately figure of Mary Wallace peering out of an upstairs window of the two-story structure. It was her favorite place, and from the description given there is no doubt that those who saw the figure were indeed seeing the ghost of Mary Wallace.

On one occasion, her intervention saved the house from burning to the ground. A heater had caught fire, but was smothered by unseen hands. The ghost has been described by one who saw her as "a lovely lady in her thirties with auburn-colored hair, smiling rather intensely and thoughtfully."

On another occasion, two state troopers saw her walking down the road leading up to the house, wearing a Colonial-type costume, and a casual visitor to the house was shown around by a tall lady at a time when the owners were away. Only later did this visitor realize that it had been Mary Wallace who had been so hospitable.

The house can be reached by car from Boston. It is worth a visit with proper permission. If you are wondering about the reality of pirates in the late eighteenth century in this area, be assured that it was not uncommon for such men of the sea to retire to their beloved New England, to settle down at a safe distance from the sea. There are other mansions and manor houses in the area which owe their existence to the wealth accumulated by sea captains, some of them of doubtful honesty, but nevertheless, if it weren't for them, these houses would have never been built. Thus we do owe Don Pedro a debt of gratitude for having caused Mary Wallace to erect this beautiful New England mansion.

26
HAUNTED MICHIE TAVERN

ichie Tavern is one of the best known attractions in historical Charlottesville, Virginia. "This typical pre-Revolutionary tavern was a favorite stopping place for travelers," the official guide of Charlottesville says. "With its colonial furniture and china, its beamed and paneled rooms, it appears much the way it did in the days when Jefferson and Monroe were visitors. Monroe writes of entertaining Lafayette as his guest at dinner here, and General Andrew Jackson, fresh from his victory at New Orleans, stopped over on his way to Washington."

The guide, however, does not mention that the tavern was moved a considerable distance from its original place to a much more accessible location where the tourist trade could benefit from it more. Regardless of this comparatively recent change of position, the tavern is exactly as it was, with everything inside, including its ghosts, intact. At the original site, it was surrounded by trees which framed it and sometimes towered over it. At the new site, facing the road, it looks out into the Virginia countryside almost like a manor house. One walks up to the wooden structure over a number of steps and enters the old tavern to the left or, if one prefers, the pub to the right, which is nowadays a coffee shop. Taverns in the eighteenth and early nineteenth centuries were not simply bars or inns; they were meeting places where people could talk freely, sometimes about political subjects. They were used as headquarters for Revolutionary movements or for invading military forces. Most taverns of any size had ballrooms in which the social functions of the area could be held. Only a few private individuals were wealthy enough to have their own ballrooms built into their manor houses.

What is fortunate about Michie Tavern is the fact that everything is pretty much as it was in the eighteenth century, and whatever restorations have been undertaken are completely authentic. I visited the allegedly haunted tavern in the company of Virginia Cloud, who lives in Charlottesville, and my psychic friend Ingrid, for whom this was a first visit to Charlottesville. Horace Burr, the eminent historian and art collector, was also one of the party.

*Haunted Michie Tavern in
Charlottesville, VA, where the sounds
of parties and duels can still be
heard, more than two Centuries after
they occured.*

Ingrid kept looking into various rooms, sniffing out the psychic presences, as it were, while I followed close behind. Horace and Virginia kept a respectable distance, as if trying not to "frighten" the ghosts away. That was all right with me, because I did not want Ingrid to tap the unconscious mind of either one of these very knowledgeable people.

Finally we arrived in the third-floor ballroom of the old tavern. I asked Ingrid what she had felt in the various rooms below. "In the pink room on the second floor I felt an argument or some sort of strife, but nothing special in any of the other rooms. I'm impressed with an argument over a woman here," Ingrid continued. "It has to do with one of the dignitaries, and it is about one of their wives."

"How does the argument end?"

"I think they just had a quick argument here, about her infidelity."

"Who are the people involved?"

"I think Hamilton. I don't know the woman's name."

"Who is the other man?"

"I think Jefferson was here."

"Try to get as much of the argument as you can."

Ingrid closed her eyes, sat down in a chair generally off limits to visitors, and tried to tune in on the past. "I get the argument as a real embarrassment," she began. "The woman is frail, she has a long dress on with lace at the top part around the neck, her hair is light brown."

"Does she take part in the argument?"

"Yes, she has to side with her husband."

"Describe her husband."

"I can't see his face, but he is dressed in a brocade jacket pulled back with buttons down the front and breeches. It is a very fancy outfit."

"How does it all end?"

"Well, nothing more is said. It is just a terrible embarrassment."

"Is this some sort of special occasion? Are there other people here?"

"Yes, oh yes. It is like an anniversary or something of that sort. Perhaps a political anniversary of some kind. There is music and dancing and candlelight."

Horace wasn't sure what it could have been, but Virginia, in great excitement, broke in here. "It was in this room that the waltz was danced for the first time in America. A young man had come from France dressed in fancy clothes. The lady he danced with was a closely chaperoned girl from Charlottesville. She was very young, and she danced the waltz with this young man, and everybody in Charlottesville was shocked: The news went around town that the young lady had danced with a man holding her, and that was just terrible at the time. Perhaps that was the occasion."

So if you feel like visiting Michie Tavern, you may or may not run into the lively party upstairs in the ballroom, but then these are fairly happy ghosts even if they shocked their contemporaries at the time.

27
THE MILLBRAE GHOST

I heard of the Millbrae case from a young girl who used to live in that house before she decided she was old enough to have a place of her own and consequently moved out to a nearby town called Burlingame. Today she is a professional spiritualist minister, a writer and a counselor. She still lives in northern California, but no longer in her parents' house.

The house was built in a most peculiar manner. Because the lot was sloping toward a ravine, the top floor reached to street level on the front side of the house only. It was here that the house had its living room and entrance hall. On the floor below were the bedrooms, and finally, a garage and adjoining work room. Underneath was a basement, which, however, led to ground level in the rear, where it touched the bottom of the ravine. When Ms. G. was a teenager she and some friends used a ouija board, more as a game than for any serious purpose. I have always been against the use of ouija boards for a variety of reasons, and I don't recommend them. When the room became very cold the girls panicked and quickly ended the session. Ever since, she heard uncanny noises in her parents' house. They ranged from footsteps to crashing sounds, as if someone or something were thrown against a wall or onto the floor. There never was a rational explanation for these sounds.

After Ms. G. moved out to her own place in Burlingame, she returned home for occasional weekends to be with her mother. One night, as she lay awake in bed, she heard footsteps overhead. They walked across the ceiling, "as if they had no place to go." Thinking that her mother was ill, she raced upstairs, but found her mother fast asleep in bed.

Once in a while, when in the dining area upstairs, she will see something out of the corner of an eye—a flash—something or somebody moving about—and as soon as she concentrates on it, it is not there. One night when she spent the weekend at her parents' house and was just falling asleep a little after midnight, she was awakened by the sound of distant voices. The murmur of the voices was clear enough but when she sat up to listen further, they went away. She went back to

sleep, blaming her imagination for the incident. But a week later, to the day, her incipient sleep was again interrupted by the sound of a human voice. This time it was a little girl's or a woman's voice crying out, *"Help . . . help me!"*

She jumped up so fast she could hear her heart beat in her ears. Surely, her mother had called her. Then she remembered that her mother had gone to Santa Cruz. There was nobody in the house who could have called for help. She looked outside. It was after midnight and the surrounding houses were all dark. But the voice she had just heard had not come from the outside. It was there, right in the haunted room with her!

Her mother said, "I hear footsteps upstairs when I'm downstairs and I hear footsteps downstairs when I'm upstairs and there is never anyone there."

A big crash also made the family wonder what was wrong with their house. Mrs. G. heard it *upstairs* and her son Allen, upstairs at the same time, thought it was *downstairs*—only to discover that it was neither here nor there!

"Many times the doorbell would ring and there was no one outside," Mrs. G. added, "but I always assumed it was the children of the neighborhood, playing tricks on us."

I visited the house with medium Sybil Leek. Through her, we learned what the haunting was all about. A man was chased into this house, a man who was actually the victim of a case of mistaken identity. This, according to the medium, happened in 1884 and his name was Wasserman. He was killed because his killers thought he was someone else. In researching the story I discovered that in 1884 there had been political irregularities and conditions in the San Francisco area had bordered on anarchy. We tried to tell the ghost that much time had gone by, and that there was no point in hanging around since his murderers had long since died off also. I also promised to tell the world by publishing a story that Mr. Wasserman was not the culprit his pursuers thought he was and that he was in fact a very nice fellow.

Things have been quiet at the house in Millbrae ever since.

28

THE HAUNTED RANCH AT NEWBURY PARK, CALIFORNIA

rs. H. is a remarkable lady, who had spent most of her life in the little town of Newbury Park, California, which is north of Los Angeles. Newbury Park has a population of about 15,000 people and its major claim to fame is its Stagecoach Inn which was once used as a stopover when the stagecoach traveled between Santa Barbara and Los Angeles, discontinued, however in 1915. The inn was moved from its old location a few years ago and is now in a more convenient place, while a major highway goes through where it once stood. The land around Newbury Park is mainly ranch land and the houses, consequently, are the ranch-style houses, low, spread out and usually painted white or gray. The H.'s live on part of what is known locally as the Hays Ranch which at one time consisted of hundreds of acres of farm land. They own two and a half acres and a small but comfortable ranch house in the middle of it. Around 1920, it appears, there was a family living in the house that had a small girl who accidently drowned in either a well or a cesspool on the property. Other than that, Mrs. H. was not aware of any tragedies having occurred in the immediate area of her house.

Mrs. H. had originally contacted me, explaining that she had problems with ghosts, without going too much into details. Now I questioned her about the goings-on in the house.

"There have been three occurrences that I have not mentioned, over the past two months. The most recent was a weird 'singing' or 'whistling' noise which I heard a few nights ago. I am reasonably sure this was not my imagination, as my

A young boy found an early death at this Newbury Park ranch house: people have seen and heard his restless ghost.

son David has told me of hearing such a noise about two months ago while he was in the bathroom. He was frightened, but no one else heard it and I could not imagine what it could be other than a little air in the pipes. But when I heard what I assume was the same noise it was while I sat up alone in our living room-kitchen.

"The other thing that happened was the day I saw the ghost. I knew from the voice that it was a boy of about 10 or 12. But his day (in late January) while I was washing the windows, I saw through the window pane clearly standing by the fence a young boy *and you could see the fence through him*! It was in the morning and that side of the house was shaded but the yard behind it was in brilliant sunlight. I wasn't sure I could believe my eyes and when I turned around he was gone.

"Another hard-to-explain event that happened was one evening at least a month ago—maybe more—when my husband and I were sitting in the living room and the room was fairly quiet. We both heard a sound that could only be called a whimpering near the door. I had heard this several months before but no one else had."

Apparently the H.'s children also had some experiences in the house. "David told me about some misty shapes he had seen, and said the other kids also saw them some time ago, in their bedroom. He said it was dark in the room and these 'things' were light. Near the ceiling he saw three misty shapes and they seemed to be looking down at the children. They were vague but he thought they were people. He called me and when I came in and opened the door they disappeared."

"The 'shapeless, horrible' thing the kids saw was on my mind for a while after that, and when I saw something in there later on, I was not sure it was not subconscious suggestion on my part and I never mentioned it to anyone, but it was about three weeks later that it happened. The children were insisting upon the door being left open and I allowed it for several weeks after they saw this thing. The night I saw *something*, the door was, therefore, open. I was sitting across from the door by the windows and looked up to see a *misty, whitish shape in the doorway* next to the partition and partly over it—above floor level, some six feet I would say.

"There hasn't been much else happening around here recently other than my hearing outdoors, apparently on the hill behind the clothesline, a whimpering sound, quite loud, that lasted for several minutes at a time.

"Also, yesterday afternoon, my daughter and I were sitting on the patio and we both heard distinctly two car doors slam on the other side of the house. She went to see if the truck doors had slammed shut, but they were both open and there were no cars out there."

Who the ghost or ghosts at Newbury Park are, I do not know. It may well be that the H.'s are simply picking up memories from the past, at least in part. But the white shapes floating into the room are had to explain on that basis. In an area which has been lived in for such a long time as this area, tragedies are bound to occur without being recorded. Perhaps someone from the past is still around, wondering who the newcomers are in what used to be his place.

29
THE NARROWSBURGH GHOST

arrowsburgh, New York lies about four hours from New York City on the Delaware River, where Pennsylvania, New York and New Jersey meet. This is a beautiful and somewhat remote area of the country, with large, open acreage and beautiful trees, and the houses, mainly farms, can be very isolated. The house in question is directly on the Delaware and had been owned by the parents of the lady who contacted me originally to investigate it, Mrs. M. of Long Island. Prior to the parents' acquisition of the house in 1942, it had been vacant for seven years and was in a run-down condition. However, it has since been restored and is used mainly on weekends by Mrs. M. and her family. The house itself is about 200 years old and much restructuring has gone on over the years. However, the foundation and the outside walls are intact and are exactly as they were when the building was first erected. On many occasions, the ghost of a woman has been seen just outside the house as though she were about to enter. This happens usually at the same hour, and with some regularity. Both Mrs. M. and her husband have actually watched for her and seen her. Also, the sound of a door closing by itself has been heard for years and Mrs. Mack has been awakened during the night many times with the feeling that someone is watching her.

One night in 1971, Mrs. M., her husband and two friends attempted a seance. For a few minutes, the room seemed to change to what it once was and Mrs. M. found herself crying uncontrollably without reason. She had the feeling that she was experiencing something that happened to a woman in 1793. In addition to the woman in distress, Mrs. M. felt a male presence as well, but from a different time period.

I asked for additional information about the house and learned that it was built in 1752 by Dutch settlers. The deed itself goes back to 1861. Narrowsburgh can be reached over Route 97. In addition, Mrs. M. explained that she had the increasing feeling that a skeleton may still be buried in the basement, but has so far not tried to dig for it. The M.'s children have also seen the apparition of the man, and Mrs. M.'s mother has felt very uneasy in certain parts of the house. Since they felt that the ghost was frightening the children, they got in touch with me in the hope I would visit and exorcise either one of the presences in their house. I agreed to visit the house in the company of my psychic friend, Ingrid Beckman, who had been an excellent medium on a number of earlier occasions. We went through the house, room by room, hoping that she would pick up some of the puzzles of the past. Within moments, Ingrid picked up the impressions of a man who was staying on after death in the northeast bedroom. Ingrid felt that the house once belonged to this man, perhaps fifty or sixty years ago, and the reason for his continued presence was that he didn't realize he was dead and considered the people he saw in his house as intruders. This is a common misconception among ghosts in general.

We then went into the cellar, an area in which Mrs. M. had felt some of the strongest vibrations. It was then that we discovered a secret room, almost concealed by the rough stones of the basement. What was this room used for, I wondered? Today it is used as a coal bin. Ingrid felt that someone was buried in that area. Now Ingrid got the entire picture more clearly. "I feel it is a woman about twenty-five years old and she was looking for some man to come to her, but he didn't show up and somehow she left the room and went down here where she was entombed. Whether she was murdered or went in there to hide, I cannot say. I feel there was a defense of the house and I sense a man with a very long rifle. This happened a long time ago. I think the woman died in this little room, either she was hiding or she couldn't get out and died there."

The house in Narrowsburgh is privately owned, and I doubt very much that visitors would be welcome.

30
THE GHOSTS OF THE OCTAGON, WASHINGTON, D.C.

 ne of the best known and most beautiful public monuments in the nation's capital is the so-called Octagon, a house built at the beginning of the 19th century in octagonal shape, thus its name. Today it is the seat of the offices of the American Institute of Architects and is maintained as a museum. It can be visited but I would advise my readers not to stress the ghosts as much as the fact that it is an historical landmark.

Originally built by orders of Colonel John Tayloe in the year 1800 as his town house in the new capital, the mansion stands in one of the most fashionable parts of Washington at the corner of New York Avenue and 18th Street. Originally it was surrounded by empty land, but today it forms the center of several avenues of mansions and expensive town houses. The Octagon contains three stories and in the downstairs part boasts a magnificent rotunda from where a staircase leads to the second and third floors. This particular staircase is the center of ghostly activities in the mansion. Most of the reported and witnessed phenomena took place on the second floor landing near the banister on the third floor and on the ground floor where a carpet keeps flinging itself back when there is no one about. Even before it was finished General Washington spent time in it and during the British occupation of the nation's capital when the White House had been burned down by the British, the Octagon served as a temporary White House to President Madison and his wife Dolly. Here Madison signed a peace treaty with Britain in 1815. After the death of Mrs. John Tayloe in 1855 the building passed into other hands and was for a time used as a school for girls. But as the neighborhood deteriorated, gradually it became a slum building. It was rescued from its unfortunate state in 1899 when the American Institute of Architects bought it and made it its headquarters.

The Octagon, briefly the temporary White House in 1812, has the added "attraction" of the ghost of Col. Tayloe's daughter, who jumped to her death when her suitor was refused by her father.

Ghostly phenomena had been reported from the Octagon as far back as the middle 19th century and include footsteps, the sound of a plaintive female voice and other unusual signs of human presences in the old mansion when no one was seen. A long list of observers have experienced psychic phenomena in the building. Of particular interest is the account of the superintendent Mr. C. who has on several occasions found the lights in the building on, after he had just turned all the switches off; on returning, he found the doors wide open where he had just locked them a few minutes before! On one occasion, Mr. C. was in the basement turning the switches off again, having been summoned to the house by the police in the middle of the night, when he clearly heard footsteps in an area he had just visited a minute before. The shock was too much for the superintendent: he almost electrocuted himself at the switches, then quickly ran up stairs only to find himself again alone in the building. The footsteps of both a man and a woman have been heard repeatedly by witnesses, especially on the second and third floors. A carpet at the bottom of the main staircase keeps flinging itself back when there is no one in the building. This is a spot immediately to the right of the staircase in the center of the downstairs hall. The chandeliers also swing of their own volition at times. Once the assistant curator heard footsteps on the third floor when she was working

on the second floor. Knowing full well that the third floor had been closed to visitors and in fact had been shut off altogether for a long time, she was puzzled as to who might be walking up and down over her head. She then tiptoed up to the third floor and looked around. There was no one to be seen, but in the dust of the floor she noticed some very light footprints, far too light to have been made by human feet and yet indicating the outlines of two delicate feet belonging to an unseen woman.

I visited the Octagon several times, twice in the company of a competent medium. The reason for the haunting goes back to the original builder of the house, stern Colonel John Tayloe. It appears that one of his daughters had fallen in love with the wrong kind of man and Colonel Tayloe would have no part of it. The daughter then committed suicide by jumping from the second floor landing. She fell and broke her neck on the very spot where the carpet keeps flinging itself back. However, this would not account for the heavy footsteps clearly belonging to a man. These are thought to be of Colonel Tayloe himself, the distraught father who had indirectly caused his daughter's death. There may, however, be a third ghost in the Octagon. During the British occupation period a young officer pursued one of the American servant girls who preferred to jump to her death rather than give in to his demands. We don't have her name, but visitors often report someone standing behind them on the upper floor. Those were the areas where the servants slept and it is to be assumed that only a servant girl would be earthbound in that area. I have made no attempt at exorcising any of these ghosts, so for all I know they may still be roaming the corridors of the Octagon.

31
THE GHOST AT OLEY FORGE

school teacher by the name of Richard S. makes his home in the heart of the Pennsylvania Dutch country. One day in 1975 I received a letter from Mr. S. reading, in part: "My wife and I live in a Colonial mansion built in 1750 by an ironmaster who was also a colonel in the American Revolution. We have reason to believe that a secret passageway was built in the vicinity of the mansion and that the home is possessed by spirits."

I promised to visit the place and investigate it. Shaner had bought Oley Forge in order to save it from vandals. It was built on the Manatawny Creek in 1744 by Colonel John Lesher, not far from Pleasantville, deep in the heart of the Pennsylvania Dutch country, equidistant from both New York City and Philadelphia.

The S.'s had restored the old house with much love and, I am sure, much expense, so that it now looks exactly the way it did when Colonel Lesher lived in it. It is a two-story stone house on a flat piece of land, with windows reaching down to the floor level the way they did in the eighteenth century. When one approaches the house, one passes an old wagon of the kind that even now can be seen in the Amish country, among people who have no use for the modern automobile. To the right of the house is an overgrown area which was once part of the gardens but has since pretty much returned to nature. There are some remnants of slave quarters and other out-buildings that the S.'s have not yet had time to restore. On the other side of the little creek and connected with the house by a narrow footbridge are the remnants of the iron works. The whole area has been subjected to a number of archeological expeditions by Mr. S. and his pupils. They have managed to discover a large number of artifacts, especially broken pottery, iron tools and glass.

The house is furnished in eighteenth-century style. Much of the furniture is authentic; the rest is new but follows the eighteenth-century model to the hilt. There are four-posters in the bedrooms, Pennsylvania Dutch chests, handmade and hand painted, and a long wooden table in the dining room which reminds one of paintings showing life in Colonial days. In one of the bedrooms there is a spinning wheel. The only modern touches are the electric light and the telephone.

"Teenagers used to call the house 'haunted' for years before we ever got

A revolutionary ghost, one time supplier of arms to George Washington's army, is said to still be residing in this old house.

here," Mr. S. explained, "and for miles around, the place had the reputation of being haunted. It had always attracted me somehow. I wondered whether it might be possible to hold a seance in the house and discover something about its past. We decided to hold it on Halloween, and I asked my students to try to fine me a good medium."

"What happened on Halloween?" I asked.

"My students were most anxious about the whole thing; we had decorated the house with candlelight. The medium, Helen Terrell, came all the way from Bethlehem, Pennsylvania."

After a while, the medium said she saw a young woman in a long gown walking through the house, weeping because she was so happy it was being restored. Next she described a well-dressed tall man coming into the sitting room and taking off his travelling coat. Then she saw a large dog with short hair, unlike any of the S.'s dogs, roaming through the house. Finally she described a lackey of very short stature walking through the center hall.

Shortly after the first seance, Mr. S. received an inquiry from an attorney in New Jersey concerning Betsy Lesher, the Colonel's last child. Apparently, there was no genealogical record of her in American literature. Sometime after receiving

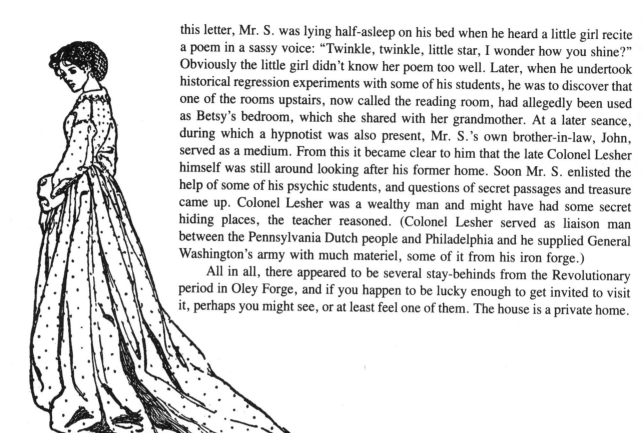

this letter, Mr. S. was lying half-asleep on his bed when he heard a little girl recite a poem in a sassy voice: "Twinkle, twinkle, little star, I wonder how you shine?" Obviously the little girl didn't know her poem too well. Later, when he undertook historical regression experiments with some of his students, he was to discover that one of the rooms upstairs, now called the reading room, had allegedly been used as Betsy's bedroom, which she shared with her grandmother. At a later seance, during which a hypnotist was also present, Mr. S.'s own brother-in-law, John, served as a medium. From this it became clear to him that the late Colonel Lesher himself was still around looking after his former home. Soon Mr. S. enlisted the help of some of his psychic students, and questions of secret passages and treasure came up. Colonel Lesher was a wealthy man and might have had some secret hiding places, the teacher reasoned. (Colonel Lesher served as liaison man between the Pennsylvania Dutch people and Philadelphia and he supplied General Washington's army with much materiel, some of it from his iron forge.)

All in all, there appeared to be several stay-behinds from the Revolutionary period in Oley Forge, and if you happen to be lucky enough to get invited to visit it, perhaps you might see, or at least feel one of them. The house is a private home.

32
THE GHOST IN THE PINK BEDROOM

he area around Charlottesville, Virginia, abounds with haunted houses, which is not surprising since this was at one time the hub of the emerging young American republic. There was a time when the American government had its capital, if only briefly, in Charlottesville and prior to the Revolution, the large landowners had built many magnificent manor houses which still dot the area. Much history and much tragedy has occurred in some of them, so it is not surprising to find that the reports of strange goings on in the area are comparatively plentiful. One such house is the property of Colonel Clark Lawrence and his family, and known as Castle Hill. It is considered one of the historical landmarks of the area and while it is not open to visitors, especially those looking for the ghost, it is conceivable that prior arrangements with the owners could be made for a student of history to have a brief visit. If this is diplomatically handled, the chances of being allowed to visit are good.

The main portion of the house was built by Dr. Thomas Walker in 1765, but additions were made in 1820. The original portion was made of wood, while the additions were of brick. These later changes executed under the direction of the new owner, Senator William Cabell Rives, gave Castle Hill its majestic appearance. Senator Rives had been American ambassador to France and was much influenced in his tastes by French architecture. This is clear when one sees the entrance hall with its twelve-foot ceilings and the large garden laid out in the traditional French manner.

On the ground floor, to the rear, there is a suite of rooms which has a decidedly feminine flavor. This is not surprising since they were the private quarters of a later owner, Amelie Rives, an author and poetess whose body lies buried in the family plot on the grounds.

In this suite there is a bedroom called the pink bedroom, which is the center of ghostly activities. Whenever guests have been assigned to sleep in this room, they invariably complain of disturbances during the night. Writer Julian Green, a

Those sleeping in the "pink bedroom" in this Virginia mansion, may be awakened by a very pretty lady ghost whose room it once was.

firm skeptic, left the next morning in great hurry. Amelie Rives herself spoke of a strange perfume in the room, which did not match any of her own scents. The ghostly manifestations go back a long time, but no one knows exactly who is attached to the room.

From the testimony of various guests, however, it appears that the ghost is a woman, not very old, rather pretty, and at times playful. Her intentions seem to be to frighten people using the room. Curiously, however, a few guests have slept in it without being aroused by uncanny noises or footsteps. Legend has it that those the lady ghost likes may sleep peacefully in "her" bedroom, while those she does not like must be frightened out of their wits.

I visited the bedroom in the company of sensitive Virginia Cloud, who had been there many times before. Curiously, I felt the vibrations of another presence, a fine, almost gentle person, but I could not see anyone. Nevertheless, I realized that I was not alone in the room, and Miss Cloud also felt that we were being observed by the unseen former owner of the place.

During the Revolutionary War, British General Banastre Tarleton and his troops occupied Castle Hill. The then owner, Dr. Walker, served them breakfast on June 4, 1781, and in the course of his hospitality delayed them as long as he could so that Jefferson, then in nearby Charlottesville, could make good his escape from the British. Whether or not one of the ladies played any significant part in this delaying action is not known, but I suspect that there is involvement of this kind connected with the appearance of the ghostly lady at Castle Hill. It was not uncommon for the women of the Revolutionary period to use their charms on the British, in order to further the cause of the revolution. Several such instances are known, and it must be said for the gallantry of the British officers, that they did not mind the intrigues of the American Colonial ladies at all.

33

THE GHOST IN THE POSTMASTER'S HOUSE

One of the most charming and at the same time historically important houses in Charlottesville, Virginia, nowadays serves as the home of the local postmaster, a man fully aware of the history all around him, who has taken excellent care of the old house. The house is known locally simply as "the Farm." Actually, it is a handsome two-story brick house, with a prominent fireplace on one end. The downstairs is now divided into two rooms—a front room very much the way it was in Colonial days, and a back room now used by the owner as a kind of storage room. Upstairs are two bedrooms. The house stands in a tree-studded lot right in the very center of Charlottesville. A little to the left of the house the postmaster pointed out the spot where the old Kings' Highway used to go through.

On the outside of the Farm, a simple plaque reminds visitors that this is one of the most historical spots in the area. Carefully avoiding any opportunity for my mediumistic friend Ingrid Beckman to see that plaque, Horace Burr, Virginia Cloud, Ingrid, and I arrived at the Farm at 3:00 in the afternoon and immediately proceeded to the main room downstairs, where Ingrid stood transfixed in front of the Colonial fireplace.

"I have the feeling that wounded people are being brought in right down here," Ingrid said. "I get the name Langdon or Langley and the name Nat." She walked around the room and then returned to her position near the fireplace. "I think the people with the light-colored breeches and the brown waistcoats and the long rifles are watching the road nearby for someone to come up that road. This is like a blockhouse, and there is some great anxiety about someone on his way up here. This is a last-ditch defense; there are perhaps five or six men, and they are upstairs with those huge rifles pointing with their long barrels and bayonets on top of them. The bullets are homemade, and it is the middle of the night. And then I get the feeling of a skirmish."

I turned to Horace Burr, asking him to comment on our observations. He seemed plainly delighted. "Well, I thought the most amazing thing that you said

was this kind of replay of a group of armed forces, a flank because there was a very interesting little maneuver that happened down the road, an attempt to cut off the main body of the armed forces coming here. The attempt went awry, though. The American troops were entrenched along the road here, expecting the British to come *this* way. Unfortunately, they came the *other* way, so the British did take Charlottesville for one night."

"What about the name Nat?"

"This house was owned at the time by Nicholas Merriweather Lewis. He was a colonel and George Washington's aide. Nat was a Colonial nickname for Nicholas."

It was on June 14, 1781, that Colonel Banastre Tarleton, the British commander, had been seen by John Jouett, who then took his famous ride to warn Jefferson and the legislature of the approaching British. When Tarleton finally got to Charlottesville later the same day, proceeding along the old Kings' Highway and destroying several wagonloads of Continental supplies on the way, he thwarted the carefully laid plans of the defenders of Charlottesville, two hundred men to whom

During the revolution, Postmaster Beagle's house of today was taken over by a group of soldiers. At times, they can still be heard arguing near the fireplace.

117

the defense of the village had been entrusted. They had been planning an ambush in the gorge below Monticello. Captain John Marson, in command of the detachment, was disappointed, but there was nothing to be done. As Tarleton entered Charlottesville, he saw the Farm, with Mrs. Lewis standing at the door, far more curious than frightened. "I think maybe I'll stay here," Tarleton is quoted as saying, and decided to make the Farm his headquarters for the night. Mrs. Lewis had heard all sorts of stories about the handsome Tarleton. The Colonel was twenty-seven and very courteous. "Madam, you dwell in a little paradise," she quoted him in her dairy.

Tarleton spent the night in front of the fireplace which had so attracted Ingrid, leaving the rest of the house to Mrs. Lewis, whose husband was away with the Continental Army.

I doubt that the ghost of Colonel Tarleton is still in the postmaster's house, but anyone lucky enough to visit there might pick up a psychic impression from the past. If there are ghosts in the house, they are not the Colonel's but perhaps some of the wounded who might have died during the skirmish between the two sides. At any rate, this is a private house and permission must be obtained from the postmaster to visit.

34
THE POUGHKEEPSIE RECTORY GHOST

few years ago Bishop James Pike made news by publicly declaring that he had spoken with his dead son James in a séance arranged on Canadian television with the late medium Arthur Ford. Not much later he himself became news when he died near the Dead Sea, having run out of gas and water in the desert. A controversial figure both in life and afterlife, Bishop James Pike, one time Bishop of California, and the author of a number of remarkable books, was no stranger to psychic phenomena.

During my work with him, I got to know the Christ Church rectory at Poughkeepsie pretty well. In 1947 Pike had been offered the position of rector, and he spent several years there. Christ Church is a large, beautiful, almost modern Episcopal church. The altar with its candles indicates what are generally called "high church" attitudes, that is, closer to Roman Catholicism. The outside of the church has remained turn-of-the-century, and so has the rectory attached immediately to the church itself. There is also a small library between the rectory and the church.

I asked permission of the rector of Christ Church to visit, and in July of 1968 I took medium Ethel Johnson Meyers there. She relived practically the entire incident Bishop Pike had reported to me privately earlier.

What had occurred during the two and a half years of James Pike's residency at Poughkeepsie was not unusual as hauntings go. To him it seemed merely puzzling, and he made no attempt to follow up on it in the way I did when I brought Mrs. Meyers to the scene. Pike had taken over his position at Poughkeepsie, replacing an elderly rector with diametrically opposed views in church matters. The former rector had died shortly afterward.

The late Bishop James Pike encountered the unhappy ghost of his predecessor in this Poughkeepsie, N.Y. rectory.

Pike soon found that his candles were being blown out, that doors shut of their own volition, and that objects overhead would move—or seemingly move—when in fact they did not. All the noises and disturbances did not particularly upset Bishop Pike. However, on one occasion he found himself faced with a bat, flying about madly in the library. Knowing that there was no way in or out of the library except by the door he had just opened, he immediately closed the door again and went to look for an instrument with which to capture the bat. When he returned and cautiously opened the door to the library, the bat had disappeared. There is no possible way by which the animal could have escaped.

Those wishing to visit Poughkeepsie can do so freely, although the rector may not be too keen to discuss psychic phenomena.

35

THE GHOST AT THE PSYCHIATRIST'S HOUSE

 first visited the sumptuous estate of Dr. and Mrs. K., the psychiatrist, because the late Florence Sternfels, prominent medium, was being tested by the doctor in the presence of a number of guests. The house is near the Hudson River and had been remodeled from an older house; at one time the building was used as a summer theatre with the current large living room used as the stage. At the time of my first visit, Mrs. K, who has had a number of ESP experiences, took me to one side and confided that she and her husband thought they had a ghost in the house. This ghost, she explained, was a very peculiar individual, for he kept whistling a certain song all the time. "During the past five years I've heard him about twenty times and he always whistles the same tune," Mrs. K. explained. What about Dr. K., I wanted to know? Mrs. K. shook her head. He didn't hear the whistling, but "he hears raps, usually in our bedroom and late at night. They always come in threes. My husband hears it, gets up and asks who it is, but of course there is nobody there so he gets no answer. Last winter around three in the morning we were awakened by a heavy knocking sound on the front door. When we got to the door to open it, there was no one in sight. The path leading up the road was empty too, and believe me no one could have come down that path and not be still visible by the time we got to the door."

The house was originally built by a certain Clifford Harmon, and was both living quarters and a summer theatre. Mr. Harmon was murdered by the Nazis during World War II, when he got trapped in France. There are many secret passageways in the house, primarily leading down to the river and perhaps also to one of the other old houses in the area. After one particularly vivid dream Mrs. K. had of such a passage, she actually found the passage which she had not known of before! There she discovered some musty old photographs of actors of both sexes.

At this point, the doctor joined the conversation, and we talked about Harmon.

"He's left much unfinished business over here, I'm sure," the doctor said. "He had big plans for building and improvements of his property, and, of course, there were a number of girls he was interested in."

I had heard enough. The classic pattern of the haunted house was all there. The ghost, the unfinished business, the willing owners. I offered to hold a "rescue circle" type of seance, to make contact with the "whistling ghost."

We decided to hold the seance on August 3rd, 1960, and that I would bring along Mrs. Meyers, since this called for a trance medium, while Florence, who had originally brought me to this house, was a clairvoyant and psychometrist. A psychometrist gets "impressions" by holding objects that belong to a certain person.

As was her custom, Ethel Johnson Meyers received some impressions about people connected with the house in the past and began to rattle off various names and describe individuals who might have lived in the house in earlier times. Suddenly both Mrs. K. and I distinctly heard the sound of heavy breathing nearby. It seemed to come from somewhere above and behind the group of the people present.

At this point full trance set in, and the medium's own personality vanished, to allow the ghost to speak to us directly, if he so chose. After a moment Albert, the medium's control, came and announced that the ghost would speak to us. Then he withdrew, and within seconds a strange face replaced the usual benign expression of Mrs. Meyer's face. This was a shrewd, yet dignified man. His voice, at first faint, grew in strength as the seconds ticked off.

"So . . . so it goes . . . Sing a Song of Sixpence . . . all over now . . ."

Excitedly Mrs. K. grabbed my arm and whispered into my ear: "That's the name of the song *he* always whistles . . . I couldn't think of it before." Through my mind went the words of the old nursery rhyme—

> Sing a Song of Sixpence,
> A pocket full of rye,
> Four and Twenty Blackbirds,
> Baked in a pie.
> When the pie was opened,
> The birds began to sing
> Isn't that a dainty dish
> To set before the king?

Like a wartime password, our ghost had identified himself through the medium.

Why did Harmon pick this song as his tune? Perhaps the gay lilt, the carefree air that goes with it, perhaps for a sentimental reason. Mrs. K. was aglow with excitement.

As I said good night to my mediumistic friend, I expressed hope that all would now be quiet at Croton.

This was wishful thinking.

The following morning, Mrs. K. telephoned me. Far from being quiet, the manifestations had increased around the house.

"We went to bed shortly after you left," she replied, "and all seemed so peaceful. Then, at 3:00 A.M., suddenly the bedroom lights went on by themselves. There is only one switch. Neither my husband nor I had gotten out of bed to turn on that switch. Nevertheless, when I took a look at the switch, it was turned down, as if by human hands!"

"Exactly one hour later, at four o'clock, the same thing happened again. By the way, do you remember the drapery covering the bedroom wall? There isn't a door or window nearby. Besides, they were all shut. No possible air current could have moved those draperies. All the same, I saw the draperies move by their own accord, plainly and visibly."

All was quiet at the K.'s, until I received another call from Mrs. K. during the last days of October.

The "Whistling Ghost" was back.

Next morning a note came from Mrs. K.

"As I told you via phone earlier this evening, we again heard our whistler last night about 1:00 A.M., and it was the loudest I have ever heard. I didn't have to strain for it. My husband heard it too, but he thought it was the wind in the chimney. Then, as it continued, he agreed that it was some sort of phenomenon. I got out of bed and went toward the sound of the whistling. I reached the den. From there I could see into the living room. Light was coming through a window behind me and was reflected upon the ceiling of the living room . . . *I saw a small white mist*, floating, but motionless, in front of the table in the living room. I called to my husband. He looked, but saw nothing. He said he would put the light on and I watched him *walk* right through the mist—he turned the lamp on and everything returned to normal."

Is the whistling ghost still around? If he is, nobody seems to mind. That's how it is sometimes with happy ghosts. They get to be one of the family.

36

THE GHOSTLY SERVANTS OF RINGWOOD MANOR

O ne of the most interesting haunted houses I ever visited is only an hour's drive from New York City, in northern New Jersey not far from Saddle River. It is a manor house known locally as Ringwood Manor and it is considered one of the more important historical houses in New Jersey. Built on land purchased by the Ogden family in 1740 it originally was the home of the owners of a successful iron smelting furnace. The area had many iron smelting furnaces during the late Colonial period when this kind of business was still profitable.

The main portion of the house dates back to 1762. Eventually it became the property of Robert Erskine, the geographer of George Washington. The local iron business soared to great heights as a result of the Revolutionary War, and the profits enabled Martin Ryerson, the later owner of Ringwood Manor, to rebuild it completely in 1807, tearing down the original old house.

However, after the iron business fell off in the 1830s, the house was sold to Peter Cooper and eventually passed to his son-in-law Abram S. Hewitt, one-time mayor of New York. Mrs. Hewitt changed the rather drab house into a mansion of fifty-one rooms, very much in the style of the early Victorian era. She moved various smaller buildings, already existing on the grounds, next to the main house, thereby giving it a somewhat offbeat appearance. In 1936, Erskine Hewitt left the estate to the state of New Jersey, and the mansion is now a museum which can be visited daily for a small fee. Not too many visitors come, however, since Ringwood Manor does not get the kind of attention some of the better-publicized national shrines attract.

I visited Ringwood Manor in the company of Ethel Johnson Meyers to follow up on persistent reports of hauntings in the old mansion. One of the chief witnesses to the ghostly goings-on was the superintendent of the manor, Alexander W. He had heard footsteps when there was no one about, footsteps of two different people, indicating two entities. Doors that had been shut at night were found standing wide open in the morning when no one human could have done it. The feeling of "presences" in various parts of the house persisted. There is a local tradition that the ghost of Robert Erskine walks about with a lantern, but there is no evidence to substantiate this legend.

As a result of my investigation and Mrs. Meyers' trance, I discovered that the restless one—at least, one of them—was a so-called Jackson White, living at the house at one time. The Jackson Whites are said to be a mixture of Negro and Indian and white. They are descendants of runaway slaves who settled in parts of New Jersey in the nineteenth century and lived among the hill folk.

The center of the hauntings seems to be what was once the area of Mrs. Erskine's bedroom, but all along the corridors both upstairs and downstairs there are spots where a sensitive person might experience chills or cold clammy feelings. I made contact with the surviving personality of Mrs. Erskine, as well as an unhappy servant whose name was Jeremiah.

Jeremiah complained bitterly about his mistress, who he claimed had mistreated him. The ghost lady whose manor we were visiting was not too pleased with our presence. Through the mouth of the medium in trance, she told us several times to get off her property! She may still be there, for all I know.

Even in death, the servants at Ringwood Manor, New Jersey, cannot rest. Their complaints can still be felt, or even heard.

37

THE HAUNTED GINGERBREAD HOUSE IN RYE, NEW YORK

ye, New York is a well-to-do suburb of New York City, no more than forty minutes by train from Manhattan, and it boasts many fine houses, some of which go back to Colonial days, but many are of the nineteenth century, and occasionally of spectacular proportions. One of these is the house in question which I visited several times in the company of both Sybil Leek and Ethel Johnson Meyers. Unfortunately, the house cannot be visited because the owners are two busy professional people, he a retired architect, she a famous portrait painter, and they have taken the ghostly presences in stride.

The house is a sprawling, mid-nineteenth century manor house standing on a bluff overlooking the New Haven Railroad. It was built around 1860 by a Jared B. Peck, and rises to four floors. There is a wide porch around it on the ground level, and the house itself stands under tall trees protecting it from the road and giving the entire estate a feeling of remoteness despite the fact that the grounds are not very large.

Downstairs there is a huge living room, filled with fine antiques tastefully matched to the period the house itself represents. In addition, there is a sitting room and a kitchen. A ghostly apparition has been seen near the kitchen, as well as on the upper stories.

The second floor contains many smaller rooms. A winding stairway leads to the third floor. Here the rooms are even smaller, since evidently that part of the house was once used as the servants' quarters. There is a sharply angled stairway

leading to the attic, closed off by a wooden door. This door has been heard to open and slam shut by itself many times.

The phenomena include opening noises of the front door, swinging of the chain when no one was about, and above all, the movement of heavy objects by their own volition. On one occasion, a carving knife took off in the well-lit kitchen and flung itself at the feet of the owners of the house as if to call attention to someone's presence. On another occasion, an ashtray flew from its place to land slowly on the floor of one of the upstairs bedrooms!

As a result of my investigations I learned that there are two different entities present—perhaps three. The door-slamming ghost may be that of a former owner,

This Victorian house in Rye, N.Y. was the scene of a small fire when a mentally deficient young woman tried to kill herself in an attic room: her ghost has been seen, and poltergeist phenomena observed here.

who spent her last years shut up in one of the small upstairs bedrooms. Perhaps she was put there by her family and resented her confinement. At any rate, there are markings on the door of one of the small bedrooms on the third floor indicating that a heavy lock must have been in place at one time.

The second entity whose presence was felt at the house goes back to the early eighteenth century and connects with an earlier house standing on the same spot. A fire is said to have consumed that earlier building, and the entity still recalls the horror of being burned.

Finally, there is a young woman who died tragically at the house in this century and whose presence may account for some of the continuing phenomena. Her signature and face appeared unexpectedly on a frame of a television film made by a crew I sent to Rye, New York, as part of a series of news programs dealing with the occult.

Mrs. S. is, as I have said, a professional portrait painter, and anyone wishing to have his or her portrait painted in her studio upstairs might very well find the sitting not quite as restful as imagined. At any rate, that is what happened to one of Molly's professional models, who was posing nude one day. Thinking that she and the painter were the only ones in the house at the time, she was surprised to find herself face to face with a woman she did not recognize. It was particularly upsetting, since the stranger disappeared almost immediately without benefit of door.

Whether this was the ghost of Mrs. W., the former owner of the house, or the young woman who appeared on film, or the girl who burned to death in the eighteenth century is hard to say.

38
SAN DIEGO'S MOST HAUNTED HOUSE

here are many old houses in southern California, some going back to the Spanish period. Quite a number of them have had ghostly manifestations. But none were as spectacular and as manifold and received as much notice as the manifestations at the Whaley House in San Diego, in a part called Old Town; a house going back only to 1857 but of great importance both historically and to ghost hunters because of the well-documented incidents which have occurred there and which are, as a matter of fact, still occurring. There is no reason to doubt that one or the other of the very active ghosts are still about the house.

The Whaley house was originally built in 1857 as a two storied mansion for a certain Thomas Whaley, one of the early pioneers of the city of San Diego, California. The house stands at the corner of San Diego Avenue and Harney Street and is nowadays kept up as a museum under the direction of Mrs. June Reading. Visitors are admitted during daylight hours and there are usually a lot of them as the fame of the house has spread throughout the United States.

There are two stories connected by a staircase. Downstairs there is a parlor, a music room, a library, and in the annex, to the left of the entrance, there used to be the County Courthouse. At least one of the hauntings is connected with the courtroom. Upstairs there are four bedrooms, tastefully furnished in the period during which the Whaley House was at its zenith—that is to say, between 1860 and 1890. The house was restored by a group of history-minded citizens in 1956. If it were not for them, there would now not be any Whaley House.

Numerous witnesses, both visitors to the house and those serving as part-time guides or volunteers, have seen ghosts here. These include the figure of a woman in the courtroom, sounds of footsteps in various parts of the house, windows opening by themselves in the upper part of the house, despite the fact that strong bolts had been installed and thus they could only be opened by someone on the inside; the figure of a man in a frock coat and pantaloons standing at the top of the stairs, organ music being played in the courtroom where there is in fact an organ

*America's most haunted house, the
Whaley House in San Diego, is still
haunted by the unhappy Mr. Whaley
who has a complaint against the city,
as well as by a couple of lesser ghosts
from the time the spot was an
execution site.*

although at the time no one was near it and the cover was closed; even a ghost dog has been seen scurrying down the hall toward the dining room. There is a black rocking chair upstairs that moves of its own volition at times, as if someone were sitting in it. A woman dressed in a green plaid gingham dress has been seen in one of the bedrooms upstairs. Smells include perfume and the scent of cigars. There is also a child ghost present, which has been observed by a number of people working in the house, and a baby has been heard crying. Strange lights, cool breezes, and cold spots have added to the general atmosphere of haunting that permeates the entire house. It is probably one of the most actively haunted mansions in the world today. The ghosts include the builder of the house, Thomas Whaley, who had a just grievance against the city of San Diego which probably has kept him tied to the house. He had put money into certain alterations so that he could sell the house to the county to be used as a courthouse. However, his contract was never executed and he was left "holding the bag." Sybil Leek pinpointed a child ghost, age twelve, by the name of Annabelle, and she also named the lady ghost upstairs correctly as Anna Lannay, Thomas Whaley's wife!

It is wise to ask for a guided tour, or at the very least to check in with Mrs. June Reading to be sure that the ghostly spots are properly pointed out. Since there are so many of them, one can hardly avoid at least one of the several hauntings at the Whaley House.

There may be an even older ghost on the premises dating to the time when the spot was used to court-martial a criminal who was hanged as a result. At that time Russian sailors came to San Diego as part of their whaling expeditions and this was truly the wild west.

Whatever the ghostly manifestations a visitor might still feel or even encounter, none of them are dangerous in the least, and there is no need to worry about any horrible experiences. The ghosts at Disneyland are more frightful.

39

THE GHOST
OF THE
SHIP CHANDLER

oving an old house from its original location to a new spot frequently awakens the ghostly manifestations which may have been slumbering in them for a long time. Such was the case when the Historical Society of Cohassett, Massachusetts moved the old ship's chandlery inland somewhat for the sake of convenience so that more tourists could visit it. Cohassett is about an hour's drive from Boston, a very old town which used to make its living mainly by the sea.

When we arrived at the wooden structure on a corner of the Post Road—it had a nautical look, its two stories squarely set down as if to withstand any gale—we found several people already assembled. Among them were Mrs. E. Stoddard Marsh, the curator of the Museum, which is what the ship's chandlery now is, and her associate, lean, quiet Robert Fraser. The others were friends and neighbors. We entered the building and walked around the downstairs portion, admiring its displays of nautical supplies ranging from fishing tackle and scrimshaw made from walrus teeth, to heavy anchors, hoists and rudders—all the instruments and wares of a ship chandler's business.

Built in the late eighteenth century by Samuel Bates, the building was owned by the Bates family, notably by one John Bates, second of the family to have the place, who had died seventy-eight years before our visit. Something of a local character, John Bates had cut a swath around the area as a gay blade. He could well afford the role, for he owned a fishing fleet of twenty-four vessels and business was good in those far-off days when the New England coast was dotted with major ports for fishing and shipping. A handwritten record of his daily catch can be seen next to a mysterious closet full of ladies' clothes. Mr. Bates led a full life.

I questioned Mrs. Marsh, the curator, about strange happenings in the house, especially after it was moved to its present site.

"Two years ago we were having a lecture here. There were about forty people listening to Francis Hagerty talk about old sailing boats. I was sitting over here to the left—on this ground floor—with Robert Fraser, when all of a sudden we heard heavy footsteps upstairs and things being moved and dragged—so I said to Mr. Fraser, 'Someone is up there; will you please tell him to be quiet'—I thought it was kids."

There was a man who had helped them with the work at the Museum who had lately stayed away for reasons unknown. Could he have heard the footsteps too and decided that caution was the better part of valor?

"The other day, just recently, four of us went into the room this gentleman occupies when he is here, and the *door closed on us* by itself. It has never done that before."

We decided to go upstairs now, and see if Mr. Bates—or whoever the ghost might be—felt like walking for us. We quietly waited in the semi-darkness upstairs, near the area where the footsteps had been heard, but nothing happened.

"The steps went back and forth," Mrs. Marsh reiterated, "heavy, masculine steps, the kind a big man would make."

A year after my visit to the Ship's Chandlery of Cohassett, nothing further was heard from the curators. Evidently John Bates must have simmered down after all. If you happen to be up near Boston and feel like visiting the house at Cohassett, do so by all means. Maybe you will be luckier than I was and John Bates will put in an appearance.

40

THE GHOSTS AT SOUTH NATICK

outh Natick is a quiet little town not far from Boston, Massachusetts with many old houses and a mixed population of Yankees and descendants of Europeans who have settled there over the years. I first heard about the place through the kindness of Mrs. Anne V., who is of part Indian descent. She contacted me at the time I was appearing on Boston television and begged me to come to what she considered a most haunted house belonging to friends of hers. What upset her more than anything else was the continual creaking of the stairs when there was no one walking on them. Also, her then four-year-old little boy showed very strange behavior whenever he entered a certain room in the house and there was an overall atmosphere of presences all over the house which disturbed the people in it. It turned out that the house had been used as a speakeasy many years ago, connected to a dance hall on the Charles River. Thus, with a checkered history, anything could have happened in a house like this.

As soon as we had investigated the creaking stairs and discovered that there was no logical reason for them to behave in such a strange manner, we were told that Anne's mother, Mrs. J., had a house nearby that was even more haunted than the one we were standing in. No sooner said than done when off we went to the other house belonging to Anne's parents.

The house itself was a gray-white, medium-sized early American house, built in the stately manner of early Georgian architecture and very well preserved. It is set back from the road a bit, framed by tall, shady trees. Built about a hundred and fifty years ago, the house has an upper story and a total of eight rooms. Bordering on the lawn of the house is a cemetery, separated from the J.'s house by an iron gate and fence.

When the J.'s moved in with their kinfolk, Mrs. J. had no thoughts of anything psychic or uncanny. She was soon to learn differently.

Upstairs, there are two bedrooms separated only by a thin wall. The larger one belongs to Mrs. J., the smaller one, to the rear of the house, is used by Roy,

In a private house in South Natick,
Massachusetts, those who once lived
in it have never left, trying to catch
the attention of the living to air their
grievances.

the husband. It was in her bedroom that Mrs. J. had another attack of the terrible feeling she had once experienced in her Canadian youth. Pinned down in her bed, it was as if someone were upon her, holding her down.

"Whose bedroom was this before you took it?" I inquired.

"Well, my daughter-in-law slept here for a while," Mrs. J. confided, "that is, before she died."

I asked further questions about this girl. At the age of 21, she had fallen ill and suffered her last agonies in this very room, before being taken off to a hospital, never to return. Her only child, to which she was naturally very attached, remained behind to be reared by Mrs. J. and Mrs. V.

Perhaps the restless spirit of the 21-year-old girl wanted some attention; or perhaps her final moments had only impressed themselves on the atmosphere of the upstairs room and were re-lived by the psychically sensitive members of the family.

41
THE SPY HOUSE GHOSTS

n June, 1696, one Daniel Seabrook, aged 26 and a planter by profession, took his inheritance of 80 pounds sterling and bought 202 acres of property from his stepfather, Thomas Whitlock. For 250 years this was a plantation in the hands of the Seabrook family who worked the land and sailed their ships from the harbor. The "spy house" is probably one of the finest pieces of Colonial architecture available for inspection in the eastern United States, having been restored meticulously over the years. The house is built in the old manner, held together with wooden pegs. They are handmade bricks, filled with clay mortar. The house has two stories and is painted white, and its sturdy construction points out the fact that the winds in the bay area can be extremely strong, strong enough to take off the roof of a house. Every room has its own fireplace as that was the only way in which Colonial houses could be heated. The house, which is located near Middletown, New Jersey, can easily be reached from New York City. It is being kept by a group headed by curator Gertrude Neidlinger, helped by her historian-brother, Travis Neidlinger, and as a museum it displays not only the furniture of the Colonial period but some of the implements of the whalers who were active in the area well into the 19th century. As an historical attraction, it is something that should not be missed by anyone, apart from any ghostly connections.

One of the rooms in the house is dedicated to the period of the Battle of Monmouth. This room, called the spy room by the British for good reasons, as we shall see, has copies of the documents kept in the Library of Congress in Washington, D.C., which are among General Washington's private papers.

In 1778, the English were marching through Middletown, pillaging and burning the village. Along the shoreline the Monmouth militia and the men who were working the whale boats got together to try and cut down the English shipping. General Washington asked for a patriot from Shoal Harbor, which was the name of the estate where the spy house is located, to help the American side fight the British. It turned out to be a certain Corporal John Stillwell, who was given a telescope and instruction to spy on the British from a hill called Garrett's Hill, not far away, the highest point in the immediate area. The lines between British and Americans were intertwined and frequently crossed one another, and it

The "Spy House" in New Jersey, a Colonial museum now, boasts a number of "stay-behinds" from the revolutionary war.

was difficult for individuals to avoid crossing them at times. The assignment given Corporal Stillwell was not an easy one, especially as some of his own relatives favored the other side in the war. Still, he was able to send specific messages to the militia who were able to turn these messages into attacks on the British fleet. At that point, Stillwell observed there were 1,037 vessels in the fleet lying off the New Jersey coastline, at a time when the American forces had no navy at all. But the fishermen and their helpers on shore did well in this phase of the Revolutionary War. John Stillwell's son, Obadiah Stillwell, 17 years old, served as message carrier from his father's observation point to the patriots. Twenty-three naval battles were fought in the harbor after the battle of Monmouth. The success of the whale boat operation was a stunning blow to the British fleet and a great embarrassment. Even daylight raids became so bold and successful that in one day two pilot boats were captured, upsetting the harbor shipping. Finally, the British gave the order to find the spy and end the rebel operation. The searching party declared the Seabrook homestead as a spy house, since they knew its owner, Major Seabrook, was a patriot. They did not realize that the real spy was John Stillwell, operating from Garrett's Hill. Nevertheless, they burned the spy house. It was, of course, later restored. Today, descendants of John Stillwell are among the society of friends of the museum, supporting it.

Gertrude Neidlinger turned to me for help with the several ghosts she felt in the house. Considering the history of the house, it is not surprising that there should be ghosts there. Miss Neidlinger herself felt someone in the entrance room, whenever she has been alone in the house, especially at night. There is also a lady in white that comes down from the attic, walks along the hall and goes into what is called the blue and white room, and there tucks the covers into a crib or bed. Then she turns and goes out of sight. Miss Neidlinger was not sure who she was, but thought she might have been the spirit of Mrs. Seabrook, who lived through the Revolutionary War in a particularly dangerous position, having relatives on both sides of the political fence.

In 1976, I brought Ingrid Beckman, my psychic friend to the spy house, which is technically located in Keensburg, New Jersey, near Middletown. Ingrid knew nothing about the place, and as she walked about it, she immediately pointed out its ancient usage as an outpost. While we were investigating the house, we both clearly heard footsteps overhead where there was no one walking. Evidently, the ghosts knew of our arrival. Without knowing anything about the history of the house, Ingrid commented, "Down here around the fireplace I feel there are people planning strategy, worried about British ships." Then she continued, "This was to mobilize something like the minutemen, farming men who were to fight. This was a strategic point because it was the entry into New York."

I then asked Ingrid to tell me whether she felt any ghosts, any residues of the past still in the house.

When we went upstairs, Ingrid tuned into the past with a bang. "There's a woman here. She ties in with this house and something about spying, some kind of spying went on here." Then she added, "Somebody spied behind the American lines and brought back information."

Upstairs near the window on the first floor landing, Ingrid felt a man watching, waiting for someone to come his way. Ingrid felt there was a man present who had committed an act of treason, a man who gave information back to the British. His name was Samuels. She felt that this man was hanged publicly.

The people call him an ex-patriot. This is the entity, Ingrid said, who cannot leave this house out of remorse. Ingrid also asserted that the house was formerly used as a public house, an inn, when meetings took place here. The curator, Miss Neidlinger, later confirmed this. Also, that among the families living in the area, most of the members served in the patriot militia, but that there were occasional traitors, such as George Taylor. Colonel George Taylor might have been the man to whom Ingrid was referring. As for the man who was hanged, it would have been Captain Huddy, and he was hanged for having caused the death of a certain Philip White. Captain Joshua Huddy had been unjustly accused of having caused the death of the patriot Philip White and despite his innocence was lynched by the patriots. Again, Ingrid had touched on something very real from history.

But the ghostly lady and the man who was hanged and the man who stared out the window onto the bay are not the only ghosts at the spy house. On the 4th of July, 1975, a group of local boys were in the house in the blue and white room upstairs. Suddenly, the sewing machine door opened by itself and the pedals worked themselves without benefit of human feet. One of the boys looked up, and in the mirror in the bureau across, he could see a face with a long beard. Another boy looked down the hall and there he saw a figure with a tall black hat and a long beard and sort of very full trousers as they were worn in an earlier age. That was enough for them and they ran from the house and never went back again. One of the ladies who assists the curator, Mrs. L., refuses to do any typing in the upstairs room because the papers will simply not stand still. A draft seems to go by all the time and blow the papers to the floor even though the windows are closed. A Mrs. B. also saw the man with the beard standing at the top of the stairs wearing a black hat and dressed in the period of the later 1700's. He had very large eyes, and seemed to be a man in his forties. He just stood there looking at her and she of course wouldn't pass him. Then he seemed to flash some sort of light back and forth, a brilliant light like a flashlight. And there were footsteps all over the house at the same time. She could even hear the man breathe, yet he was a ghost!

42
THE GHOSTS AT STAMFORD HILLS

T he 1780 House, so named because of the large date 1780 over the door just beneath the American eagle is one of the finer Colonial houses in the Stamford, Connecticut area. At the time of this story it was owned and lived in by Mr. and Mrs. Robert C., an advertising executive who had an open mind about such things as ghosts. The house has three levels and the C.'s used for their dining room the large room next to the kitchen in what today might be called ground level or even cellar. On the next level was a living room and a kind of sitting room. Beyond that there was a corridor leading to the master bedroom and a den. Upstairs there were two guest rooms and a small attic accessible only through a hole in the ceiling. The house had been built during the American Revolution, standing on a wooded slope and was originally called the Woodpecker Ridge Farm, Stamford, Connecticut. The C.'s later moved to New York City and are presently living in Atlanta, Georgia. They did not sell the house because of the ghosts in it, but because they wanted to be more in the center of a large city.

As soon as we had settled ourselves in front of one of the comfortable fireplaces I asked Mr. C. to recount his experiences in the old house. At the time they had been in the house nearly ten years.

"From time to time (once a week or so) during most of the time we've lived here I have noticed unidentifiable movements out of the corner of my eye . . . day or night. Most often, I've noticed this while sitting in our parlor and what I see moving seems to be in the living room. At other times, and only late at night when I am the only one awake, I hear beautiful but unidentified music seemingly played by a full orchestra, as though a radio were on in another part of the house.

Staircase where ghost steps were heard.

"The only place I recall hearing this is in an upstairs bedroom and just after that I'd gone to bed. Once I actually got up, opened the bedroom door to ascertain if it was perhaps music from a radio accidently left on, but it wasn't.

"Finally, quite often I've heard a variety of knocks and crashes that do not have any logical source within the structural set-up of the house. A very loud smash occurred two weeks ago. You'd have thought a door had fallen off its hinges upstairs, but, as usual, there was nothing out of order.

"My wife had two very vivid experiences about five years ago. One was in the kitchen, or rather outside of a kitchen window. She was standing at the sink in the evening and happened to glance out the window when she saw a face glaring in at her. It was a dark face but not a Negro, perhaps Indian; it was very hateful and fierce.

"At first she thought it was a distorted reflection in the glass but in looking closer, it was a face glaring directly at her. All she could make out was a face only and as she recalls it, *it seemed translucent*. It didn't disappear, *she did!*

"On a summer afternoon my wife was taking a nap in a back bedroom and was between being awake and being asleep when she heard the sounds of men's voices and the sound of working on the grounds—rakes, and garden tools—right outside of the window. She tried to arouse herself to see who they could be, but she couldn't get up."

As the quietness of the countryside slowly settled over us, I could indeed distinguish faraway, indistinct musical sounds, as if someone were playing a radio underwater or at great distance. A check revealed no nearby house or parked car whose radio could be responsible for this.

After a while we got up and looked about the room itself. We were standing about quietly admiring the furniture, when both my wife and I, and of course the C.'s, clearly heard footsteps overhead. We decided to assemble upstairs in the smaller room next to the one in which we had heard the steps. The reason was that Mrs. C. had experienced a most unusual phenomenon in that particular room.

"It was like lightning," she said, "a bright light suddenly come and gone."

I looked the room over carefully. The windows were arranged in such a manner that a reflection from passing cars was out of the question. Both windows, far apart and on different walls, opened into the dark countryside away from the only road.

Catherine and I sat down on the couch, and the C.'s took chairs. We sat quietly for perhaps twenty minutes, without lights except for a small amount of light filtering in from the stairwell. It was very dark, certainly dark enough for sleep and there was not light enough to write by.

As I was gazing towards the back wall of the little room and wondered about the footsteps I had just heard so clearly, I saw a blinding flash of light, white light, in the corner facing me. It came on and disappeared very quickly, so quickly in fact that my wife, whose head had been turned in another direction at the moment, missed it. But Mrs. C. saw it and exclaimed, "There it is again. Exactly as I saw it."

Despite its brevity I was able to observe that the light cast a shadow on the opposite wall, so it could not very well have been an hallucination.

I decided it would be best to bring Ethel Johnson Meyers to the house, and we went back to New York soon after.

Actually two visits with Meyers were necessary to clarify the situation. The story was this: a young girl by the name of Lucy, born in 1756, had been in love with a young man named Benjamin. Her grandfather Samuel had killed Benjamin by throwing him down a well in back of the house in 1774. The name Harmon was mentioned. The young man allegedly was buried on the hill and the grandfather was buried to the west of a white structure on the same grounds. The tombstone allegedly was broken off at the top. This, according to the medium, was done by vandals.

The fascinating part of all this is that the Stamford, Connecticut Historical Society and some of their volunteer student helpers were given permission to dig around the historical house and grounds not much later. Picture everyone's surprise when they came up with a tombstone with the name Samuel on it, broken off at the top. The house is privately owned and I very much doubt that it can be easily visited.

43

THE HAUNTED SUMMER THEATRE

ummer theatres do not always come as regular theatre buildings, often they are improvised in existing buildings, such as barns, rustic houses, and even churches. So long as the plays chosen by the actors are not controversial or offensive to the beliefs of the particular church who is their landlord, no trouble is likely to occur. Nowadays, even somewhat daring plays are put on in churches because our sense of what is morally acceptable has undergone major changes in the last few years. But when a church housing a summer theatre is also host to a ghost, the matter becomes somewhat more complicated. This is especially so when the church, or rather its minister, has a closed mind on the subject of hauntings and ghosts, and fears that mentioning such goings-on might hurt his religious prowess. That this is not so can be readily seen, because the phenomena exist independent of what denomination the church belongs to. In the foregoing story the phenomena are totally unconnected with the church itself and are the results of its usage as a theatre rather than as a religious building.

Not far from Thousand Oaks, California stands a simple wooden church called Missionary Baptist Church. It is situated on a small bluff overlooking the freeway access road. This church is actually an old dairy barn remodeled, first into a theatre, and later, when the theatre people left, into the present church. (The original owner, a Mr. Goebel, sold it to the Conejo Valley Players, an amateur theatrical group.) There is a large door in front, and a smaller one in the rear, by which one can now gain access to the church. There is also an attic, but the attic is so low that no one can possibly stand up in it. This is of importance, since the observed hautings seem to have emanated from that attic. Footsteps have been heard overhead by some of the Conejo Valley Players, when there was positively

*Now a church, this was once a
summer theatre at Thousand Oaks,
California. An actor died there
tragically . . . and I don't mean on
stage.*

no one overhead. If there had been anyone standing in the attic, he would have had to have been no more than three feet tall. No flesh and blood person can stand up in the attic. What was once the stage of Conejo Valley Players is now the area of the altar. The minister of the Baptist church does not take kindly to psychic phenomena, so a visitor must make his own arrangements or simply walk into the church—for worship, as it were—and further such psychic impressions as he or she can without causing any stir.

The phenomena consisted mainly of a man's footsteps. Someone was pacing up and down in the attic. At first, no one paid any attention to it, trying to pretend the noise was not real. Eventually, however, members of the audience kept asking what the strange goings-on over their heads meant. Was there another auditorium there? Sometimes it sounded as if heavy objects such as furniture were being moved around. There was of course nothing of the kind in the attic.

One young girl, who had not been a member of the troupe for long, became almost hysterical and insisted that someone had been murdered in the building. Two ladies with psychic leanings could never enter the structure without immediately getting cold, clammy feelings. These feelings mounted and turned into terror when they attempted to go up into the attic, and, on hands and knees, look around for the cause of the strange noises.

Hurriedly, they went down again. The noises continued, not only at night during actual performances, but even in the afternoons during rehearsals or casual visits.

Sybil Leek stuck her head into the attic immediately when we entered the barn. To her, that was the place of the haunting, although I had not told her anything whatever about the problem. Serious-faced, she walked about the barn for a while, again poked her head into the attic, standing on a few steps leading up to it and then shook her head. She explained that the young man who had been murdered there would not leave.

Of course the barn is no longer a theatre, but a church. This, however, does not seem to make the slightest difference to the ghost who lives in the past, his own past that is, to whom the outside world simply does not exist. If you are fortunate enough to visit this barn, just ask for the barn by name and location and you *may* be rewarded with a psychic experience.

44

MRS. SURRATT'S GHOST AT FORT MCNAIR

ort McNair is one of the oldest military posts in the United States and has had many other names. First it was known as the Arsenal, then called the Washington Arsenal, and in 1826 a penitentiary was built on its grounds, which was a grim place indeed. Because of disease, President Lincoln ordered the penitentiary closed in 1862, but as soon as Lincoln had been murdered, the penitentiary was back in business again.

Among the conspirators accused of having murdered President Lincoln, the one innocent person was Mrs. Mary Surratt, whose sole crime consisted of having run a boarding house where her son had met with some of the conspirators. But as I have shown in a separate investigation of the boarding house in Clifton, Maryland, her son John Surratt was actually a double-agent, so the irony is even greater. She was the first woman hanged in the United States, and today historians are fully convinced that she was totally innocent. The trial itself was conducted in a most undemocratic manner, and it is clear in retrospect that the conspirators never had a chance. But the real power behind the Lincoln assassination, who might have been one of his own political associates, wanted to make sure no one was left who knew anything about the plot, and so Mary Surratt had to be sacrificed.

There is a small, ordinary looking building called Building 21 at Ft. McNair, not far from what is now a pleasant tennis court. It was in this building that Mary Surratt was imprisoned and to this day sobs are being heard in the early hours of the morning by a number of people being quartered in the building. The penitentiary stands no more and the land itself is now part of the tennis court. Next to building 21 is an even smaller house, which serves as quarters for a number of officers. When I visited the post a few years ago, the Deputy Post Commander was quartered there. Building 20 contains five apartments which have been remodeled a few years ago. The ceilings have been lowered, the original wooden floors have been replaced with asbestos tile. Unexplained fires occurred there in the mid 1960's. The execution of the conspirators, including Mrs. Mary Surratt, took place

*The house where Mary Surrat spent
her last hours prior to being executed
still stands on the grounds of Ft.
McNair in Washington, D.C.
Evidently she never quite left there.*

just a few yards from where Building 21 now stands. The graves of the hanged conspirators were in what is now the tennis court, but the coffins were removed a few years after the trial and there are no longer any bodies in the ground.

Captain X.—and his name must remain secret for obvious reasons—had lived in apartment number five for several years prior to my interviewing him. He has not heard the sobbing of Mary Surratt but he has heard a strange sound, like high wind.

However, Captain and Mrs. C. occupied quarters on the third floor of Building 20 for several years until 1972. This building, incidentally, is the only part of the former penitentiary still standing. The C.'s apartment consisted of the entire third floor and it was on this floor that the conspirators, including John Wilkes Booth, who was already dead, were tried and sentenced to die by hanging. Mary Surratt's cell was also located on the third floor of the building. Mrs. C. has had ESP experiences before, but she was not quite prepared for what occurred to her when she moved onto the post at Ft. McNair.

"My experiences in our apartment at Ft. McNair were quite unlike any other I have ever known."

On several occasions, very late at night, someone could be heard walking above, yet we were on the top floor. One night the walking became quite heavy, and a window in the room which had been Mrs. Surratt's cell was continually being rattled, as if someone were trying to get in or out, and there seemed to be a definite presence in the house. This happened in April, as did the trial of the conspirators.

I doubt that it would be easy to visit Ft. McNair for any except official reasons, such as perhaps an historical investigation. But for better or for worse the building in question is located on the northeast corner of the tennis courts and Ft. McNair itself is in Washington, D.C., at the corner of Fourth and P Street and easy to reach from the center of the city.

45

THE GHOST ON TENTH STREET

ctually this ghost doesn't haunt Tenth Street, New York City, but the church that stands on the corner of Tenth Street and Second Avenue known as St. Mark's-in-the-Bowery. St. Mark's, a Dutch reformed church, is one of the most famous landmarks in New York City. It was built in 1799 on the site of an earlier chapel going way back to Peter Stuyvesant who was governor of New York in the year 1660. As a matter of fact, Governor Stuyvesant, who become the legendary Father Knickerbocker, himself is buried in the crypt. The last member of his family died in 1953 and then the crypt was sealed. One can see the crypts from across the street because they are half underground and half above ground, making the churchyard of St. Mark's-in-the Bowery a unique sight. The church itself suffered a fire not long ago, allegedly due to a cigarette left by a negligent worker working on the steeple restorations. Whether the fire was of natural origin or in some way connected with the paranormal goings on in the church is debatable but as soon as the charred remains of the roof had been removed, rebuilding on St. Mark's-in-the Bowery got started, and today it is again what it was before the fire. Built along neo-classical lines it stands in an area which is essentially an economically poor neighborhood. At one time, of course, this was not so. Around the church and the cemetery is a cast iron fence and the church is open most of the time, although one should look at the schedule to see when visitors are permitted, since various neighborhood happenings such as concerts and meetings also use the church. When the church is open to the public, one need not get permission from anyone to visit it.

St. Mark's boasts of three known ghosts. First there is a woman parishioner who has been observed by a number of reputable witnesses in the middle of the nave, staring at the altar. She has been described as a Victorian woman, very pale and apparently unhappy. Who she is nobody seems to know. Another ghost has been observed on the balcony close to the magnificent organ. Several organists have had the uncanny feeling of being observed by someone they could not see. One of the men working in the church reported hearing footsteps coming up to the organ loft. He assumed that the organist had come to work early and got ready to welcome him when to his surprise the footsteps stopped and total silence befell the

The Dutch Reformed church on 10th Street, New York City, has a couple of interesting ghosts: an organist who keeps walking up to the organ (which is long gone) and a lady parishioner who materializes in the nave, not to mention Old Father Knickerbocker himself, who lies buried below in the crypt—Peter Stuyvesant.

organ loft. Needless to say, he did not see any organist. Finally, there are those who have heard the sounds of a man walking distinctly with a cane and it is thought that the limping ghost is none other than Peter Stuyvesant himself, who, as we know, had a wooden leg and used a cane. His body, after all, lies in the crypt beneath the church.

St. Mark's-in-the Bowery is easy to reach by bus or subway, with a short walk from either the Eastside Lexington Avenue Subway or the BMT. It is advisable to go there during the daytime, because the area is not entirely free from some of the less desirable characters drifting in from the nearby Bowery and also because it is generally closed at night.

46

THE
HAUNTED
TRAILER

utside Boston at Peabody, Massachusetts in a trailer park lives a lovely lady of Austrian descent by the name of Rita Atlanta. That is not her real name, to be sure, but the name under which she dances in nightclubs. Rita came to America at an early age after undergoing some horrifying experiences at the hand of occupying Russian troops in her native Austria. She became a well-known dancer in nightclubs both in this country and in Europe and it was in Frankfurt, Germany where we first met. At that time she had read one of my books and had explained to me that she needed some advice concerning a ghostly apparition in her trailer. It seems unusual to hear about ghosts in so modern a residence as a trailer camp but I have heard of ghosts in airplanes and in modern apartment buildings, so I was not particularly surprised.

We spent about an hour talking about Miss Atlanta's other ESP incidents, of which she had a number over the years, and looked at her album of show business photographs, showing her in her "speciality"—which was appearing inside a large wine glass.

But whenever Rita did not travel on business, she and her teenage son lived in a trailer outside Boston. Sometimes they spent months at a time there when things were slow in the nightclub business. The boy went to school nearby, being looked after by the grandmother. The trailer itself is fairly large and looks no different from any other trailers of this type, that is to say trailers that are not likely to travel anywhere but are put on a firm base in a camp and are expected to remain there. The sides are made of metal and inside the trailer there is a large bedroom, a dining room, a kitchen and a small room, almost the same as if this were a conventional small apartment. To be sure, space is tight, but it seemed a comfortable home to me when I visited it a little later.

The reason Miss Atlanta was upset by the goings-on in her trailer had to do with something that happened night after night, at 3:00 in the morning. She would wake from deep sleep to see a man, wearing a dark overcoat, standing in front of

Rita Atlanta, the owner at the time of the haunting, in front of her trailer.

A man was run over near this haunted trailor in Peabody, Massachusetts, but is evidently unaware of his death.

her bed and staring at her. She could not make out his face nor could she see his feet, yet there was no mistaking the tall figure of a man coming out of nowhere without the benefit of doors opening, and clearly for reasons of his own. It did not frightened Rita for she had had psychic experiences before. But she began to wonder why this stranger kept appearing to her in what she knew was a new trailer, having bought it herself a few years prior. Even her son saw the stranger on one occasion. So she knew that it was not her active imagination causing her to see things.

She began to ask questions of neighbors, people living in other trailers in the camp. Finally she came upon an assistant to the manager of the camp who had been there for a long time. He nodded seriously when she described what was occurring in her trailer. Then he showed her a spot on the road just in front of it, explaining that it was there where she would find the cause of her problem. Some years before a man roughly fitting the description she had given had been run over and killed by a car. Clearly then, Rita Atlanta figured, the apparition she had seen in her trailer was that of the restless spirit of the man who had died in front of it and was confused as to his true status. Whenever his spirit recalled the moment of his untimely death, he apparently had felt a compulsion to look for help and the nearest place to look would have been her trailer.

Ever since Rita and I discussed this over coffee in her trailer, the apparition has not returned.

47

THE GHOST
AT WEST POINT

o much history has taken place at the Military Academy at West Point, which used to be a fortress guarding the approaches of the Hudson River, it is not surprising that ghostly apparitions should have also occurred from time to time.

Four military cadets at the United States Military Academy saw the apparition of a soldier dressed in eighteenth century cavalry uniform, and according to the witnesses, the apparition seemed luminous and shimmering. Apparently, the ghost materialized out of the wall and a closet in room 4714 and on one occasion also from the middle of the floor. Once it ruffled the bathrobe of a cadet, and on another occasion it turned on a shower!

As soon as the publicity drew the attention of the guiding spirits (of the military kind) to the incident, room 4714 was emptied of its inhabitants. The room itself was then declared off-limits to one and all. Ghosts, of course, do not obey military authorities. Cadet Captain Keith B., however, was willing to discuss it intelligently. "There is no doubt about it at all," he said, "the room grew unnaturally cold." Two weeks before, he and another upperclassman spent a night sleeping in the room, their beds separated by a partition. At about 2:00 in the morning Cadet B's companion began to shout. He jumped from his bed and rounded the partition, but he could not see anything special. What he did feel, however, was an icy cold for which there was no rational explanation.

However, he and his companion weren't the first ones to encounter the ghost. Two plebes who occupied room 4714 before them also saw it. The second time the apparition walked out of the bureau that stood about in the middle of the floor. He heard the plebes shout, and ran into the room. One of the cadets who actually saw the apparition was able to furnish a drawing. It is the face of a man with a drooping moustache and a high old-fashioned cap surmounted by a feather. It is the uniform of a cavalry man of about two hundred years ago.

West Point has a number of ghostly legends, what is now the superintendent's mansion allegedly has a 150 year old ghostly girl, a woman named Molly, who in life was a sort of camp follower.

Another cadet was taking a shower, prior to moving into the haunted room on the same floor and on leaving the shower noticed that his bathrobe was swinging

The ghost at West Point military academy is not welcome to authorities there, but has nevertheless been observed by many: he is a plebe who committed suicide.

back and forth on the hook. Since the door was closed and the window closed, there could be no breeze causing the robe to move. The building in which this occurred stands on old grounds; an earlier barrack stood there which has long since been demolished. Could it be that the ghostly cavalry man might have died there and been unable to adjust to his new surroundings.

If you visit West Point, try to find the building that contains room 4714. Company G-4 is quartered there, and perhaps someone will help you find the way.

48
THE VINELAND GHOST

ancy, an attractive blonde and her handsome husband Tom moved into the old farm house near Vineland, New Jersey in the summer of 1975. Tom had been a captain in the Air Force when he and Nancy met and fell in love in her native Little Rock, Arkansas. After three years, Tom decided he wanted to leave his career as a pilot and settle down on a farm. They returned to Tom's hometown of Vineland, where Tom got a job as the supervisor of a large food processing company.

The house had been built in 1906 by a family named Hauser who had owned it for many generations until Tom's father acquired it from the last Hauser nineteen years before. Sitting back a few hundred yards from the road, the house has three stories and a delicate turn of the century charm. There is a porch running the width of the front, and ample rooms for a growing family. Originally there were 32 acres to the surrounding farm but Tom and Nancy decided they needed only four acres to do their limited farming. Even though the house was very run down and would need a lot of repair work, Tom and Nancy liked the quiet seclusion and decided to buy it from Tom's father and restore it to its former glory.

"The first time I walked into this house I felt something horrible had happened in it," Nancy explained to me.

By the time the family had moved in Nancy had forgotten her initial apprehension about the house. But about four weeks later the first mysterious incident occurred.

As Nancy explained it, "I was alone in the house with the children whom I had just put to bed. Suddenly I heard the sound of children laughing outside. I ran outside to look but didn't see anyone. I ran quickly back upstairs but my kids were safely in their beds, sound asleep, exactly where I'd left them."

That summer Nancy heard the sound of children laughing several times, always when her own were fast asleep. Then one day Nancy discovered her daughter Leslie Ann, then aged three-and-a-half, engaged in lively conversation

This Vineland, N.J. house has the ghost of Emma, once its owner, to account for the many strange goings-on that have created problems for the new owners.

with an unseen friend. When asked what the friend looked like, the child seemed amazed her mother couldn't see her playmate herself.

Convinced they had ghostly manifestations in the house, they decided to hold a seance with the help of a friend. After the seance the phenomenon of the unseen children ceased but something else happened—the gravestone incident.

"We found the gravestone when we cleared the land," Tom said. "We had to move it periodically to get it out of the way. We finally left it in the field about a hundred yards away from the house. Suddenly the day after our seance it just decided to relocate itself right outside our back door. It seemed impossible—it would have taken four strong men to move that stone.

For some time Nancy had the uncanny feeling that Ella Hauser, the woman who had built the house was "checking" on the new occupants. Tom had looked on the ghostly goings-on in a rather detached, clinical way, but when his tools started disappearing it was too much for even him.

Tom and Nancy were not the only ones who encountered the unknown. In August of 1977, a babysitter, Nancy F., was putting the children to bed, when she heard someone going through the drawers downstairs. "She thought it was a

prowler looking for something," Nancy explained, "But when she finally went downstairs nothing had been touched."

The night after the babysitter incident Nancy went downstairs to get a drink of water and found a five-foot ten inch tall man standing in her living room—at 3:00 in the morning.

"He was wearing one of those khaki farmer's shirts and a pair of brown work pants. Everything was too big for the guy. I could tell he was an old man. I took one look and ran upstairs."

When I received their telephone call I immediately asked for additional details. It became clear to me that this was a classical case of haunting where structural changes, new owners and new routines have upset someone who lived in the house and somehow remained in the atmosphere. As is my custom, I assembled the residents and a psychic I had brought with me into an informal circle in the kitchen. Together we asked Ella and whoever else might be "around" to please go away in peace and with our compassion—to enter those realms where they would be on their own. The atmosphere in the kitchen, which had felt rather heavy until now, seemed to lift.

When I talked to Nancy several weeks after my visit, all was well at the house.

The house is privately owned and I doubt that the Jones are receiving visitors. But you can drive by it, most people in Vineland, New Jersey know which one it is.

49

A VIRGINIA HAUNTED HOUSE

ost people think of Vienna being in Austria but there is an equally lovely though much smaller Vienna located in Virginia, not far from Washington, D.C. This quiet community boasts a number of lovely old houses among them one belonging to Mrs. Lucy D. at the time when I visited it.

When we arrived at the D.'s House, I was immediately impressed by the comparative grandeur of its appearance. Although not a very large house, it nevertheless gave the impression of a country manor—the way it was set back from the road amid the trees, with a view towards a somewhat wild garden in the rear. A few steps led up to the front entrance. We entered a large living room that led to a passage into a dining room and thence into the kitchen. In the center of the ground floor is a staircase to another floor, and from the second floor, on which most of the bedrooms are located, there is a narrow staircase to a garret that contains another bedroom.

The house was beautifully furnished in late Colonial style, and antiques had been set out in the proper places with a display of taste not always met these days.

"What made you think there was something unusual about the house after you moved in?" I asked Mrs. D.

"I was about the last member of the family to be aware that something was going on, but I had heard repeated stories from the children. I was sleeping in one of the children's rooms upstairs one night, and was awakened by heavy footsteps—not in the room but in the next room. I wondered who was up, and, I heard them walking back and forth and back and forth. I finally went back to sleep, but I was kind of excited. The next morning I asked who was up during the night, and no one had been up."

"What was the next thing?"

"I was sleeping in my son Douglas' room again, and I was having a very frightening dream. I don't remember what the dream was, but I was terrified. Suddenly I awoke and looked at the wall. Before I had gone off to sleep, I had noticed that the room had been sort of flooded with panels of light, and there were two shafts of light side by side, right directly at the wall. I sat right up in bed and I looked up and there was the *shadow of a head*. I don't know whether it was a man's or a woman's, because there were no features, but there was a neck, there was hair, it was the size of a head, and it was high up on the wall. It could have been a woman with short, bushy hair. It was so real that I thought it was Joyce, my daughter, who was about eighteen then. I said, 'Joyce,' and I started speaking to it. Then I realized it was waving a little bit. I became frightened. After about ten minutes of saying, 'Joyce, Joyce, who is it? Who is there?' it moved directly sideways, into the darkness and into the next panel of light, and by then I was crying out, 'Joyce, Joyce, where are you?' I wanted someone to see it with me."

"What was the next event that happened after that?"

"In nineteen sixty-seven we decided to get a Ouija board. We had some friends who knew this house well, and said, 'You ought to work a board and find out what was there.' They owned this house for about ten or fifteen years; their names are Dean and Jean.

"On several occasions they heard a woman talking in the kitchen when there was no other woman in the house. They heard the voice, and they also heard the heavy garage doors bang up and down at night, with great noise."

"What did you decide to do after that?" Apparently, the D.'s decided to use the time honored Ouija board to find out who was causing all the problems. Immediately they received the names of two people, Martha and Morgan.

"Martha said that it was *she* who was appearing on the wall, because one child in the next room had fallen out of bed, and Martha loves children, and tried to help. And Martha said dear things about me—that I have a big job, and it's hard for me to handle the children, and she's here to help."

"Does she give you any evidence of her existence as a person?"

"I think she and Morgan are brother and sister and they're both children of Sarah. And Sarah was the first wife of Homer Leroy Salisbury who built this house in eighteen sixty-five."

Apparently a lot of the phenomena started when structural changes were made in the house, altering its appearance from what it was in the nineteenth century. Even people who stay at the house who are not members of the family soon come face to face with the ghost or at least one of them.

"A friend, Pat Hughes, saw a woman here one night. Pat was here with a man named Jackson McBride, and they were talking, and at 3:00 I left and went to bed. At about 4:00 in the morning, Pat heard noises in the kitchen and thought I had gotten up. She heard someone walking back and forth. Pat was over there, and said, 'Come on in, Lucy, stop being silly. Come in and talk to us.' And this apparition walked in, and then Pat said, 'It's not Lucy'—she realized that the ghost looked similar to me. It was tall and slim, had long dark hair, and had a red robe on and something like a shawl collar, and her hand was holding the collar. Pat was excited and said, 'My God, it's not Lucy! *Who is it?*' She said to this man, 'Come and look,' but he was afraid. Then Pat turned to go back and try to communicate, but it had vanished! Later, they heard a great rattle of things in the kitchen."

Several months later I returned to the house in the company of Ethel Johnson Meyers. That's when we met another spirit named Emma, connected with the house. Someone named Leon had apparently killed her. We tried to assure the restless spirits they need not hang around the house any longer and to go into the next state of existence. Apparently this worked, for I heard again from Lucy several months later, and she assured me that things in the house had become completely quiet. However, she had decided to sell the house after all, to move to a smaller apartment.

If you happen to be in Vienna, Virginia, and somehow manage to be allowed inside the former D.'s homestead, you are likely to meet up with at least one if not several of the resident ghosts, because I have the feeling that we haven't dispatched them all, if any.

50
THE HAUNTED ORGAN AT YALE UNIVERSITY

ale University in New Haven, Connecticut is an austere and respectable institution, not taking such matters as ghostly manifestations very lightly. I must therefore keep the identity of my informant a secret, but anyone who wishes to visit Yale and admire its magnificent historical organ is of course at liberty to do so, provided he or she get clearance from the proper authorities. I would suggest, however, that the matter of ghostly goings-on not be mentioned at such a time. If you happen to experience something out of the ordinary while visiting the organ, well and good, but let it not be given as the reason to the university authorities for your intended visit.

I first heard about this unusual organ in 1969 when a gentleman who was then employed as an assistant at Yale had been asked to look after the condition and possible repairs of the huge organ, a very large instrument located in Woolsey Hall. This is the fifth largest organ in the world and has a most interesting history.

Woolsey Hall was built as part of a complex of three buildings for Yale's two hundredth anniversary in 1901 by the celebrated architects, Carere and Hastings. Shortly after its completion the then university organist, a Mr. Harry B. Jepson succeeded in getting the Newberry family of the famous department store clan to contribute a large sum of money for a truly noble organ to be built for the hall. Even in 1903 this was considered to be an outstanding instrument because of its size and range. By 1915 certain advances in the technology of pipe organs made the 1903 instruments somewhat old fashioned. Again Jepson contacted the

Newberry family about the possibility of updating their gift so that the organ could be rebuilt and the hall enlarged. This new instrument was then dedicated in 1916 or thereabouts. By 1926 musical tastes had again changed further toward romantic music and it became necessary to make certain additions to the stops as well as the basic building blocks of the classical ensemble. Once again the Newberry family contributed toward the updating of the instrument. The alterations were undertaken by the Skinner Organ Company of Boston, in conjunction with an English expert by the name of G. Donald Harrison. Skinner and Harrison did not get on well together and much tension was present when they restored and brought up to date the venerable old organ.

Professor Harry Jepson was forced to retire in the 1940's, against his wishes, and though he lived down the street only two blocks from Woolsey Hall, he never set foot again into it to play the famous organ which he had caused to be built. He died a bitter and disappointed man sometime in 1952. The last university organist, Frank Bozyan, retired five years ago with great misgivings. He confided to someone employed by the hall that he felt he was making a mistake; within six months after his retirement he was dead. As time went on, Woolsey Hall, once a temple of beauty in the fine arts, was being used for youth programs involving rock and roll groups and mechanically amplified music. Undoubtedly those connected with the building of the hall and the organ would have been horrified at the goings-on, had they been able to witness them.

A gentleman who brought all of this to my attention, and who shall remain nameless, had occasion to be in the hall and involved with the organ itself on many a day. He became aware of a menacing and melancholic sensation in the entire building, particularly in the basement and the organ chambers. While working at odd hours late in the night there, he became acutely aware of some sort of unpleasant sensation just murking around the next corner or even standing behind him! On many occasions he found it necessary to look behind him in order to make sure he was alone. The feeling of a presence became so strong he refused to be there by himself, especially in the evenings. Allegedly, the wife of one of the curators advised him to bring a crucifix whenever he had occasion to go down to the organ chambers. She also claimed to have felt someone standing at the entrance door to the basement, as if to keep strangers out.

I visited Yale and the organ one fine summer evening in the company of my informant, who has since then found employment elsewhere. I too felt the oppressive air in the organ chambers, the sense of a presence whenever I moved about. Whether we are dealing with the ghost of the unhappy man who was forced to retire and never set foot again into his beloved organ chamber, or whether we are dealing with an earlier influence, is hard to say. Not for a minute do I suggest that Yale University is haunted or that there are any evil influences concerning the university itself. But it is just possible that sensitive individuals visiting the magnificent organ at Woolsey Hall might pick up some remnant of an unresolved past.

51
AMITYVILLE, AMERICA'S BEST KNOWN HAUNTED HOUSE

he night of Friday, November the thirteenth, 1974, six members of the DeFeo Family of Amityville, Long Island, were brutally murdered in their beds—one of the most horrifying and bizarre mass murders of recent memory.

The lone survivor of the crime, Ronald DeFeo Jr. who had initially notified police, was soon after arrested and formally charged with the slayings. But there are aspects to the case that have never been satisfactorily resolved.

When Ronald DeFeo Jr. got up in the middle of the night, took his gun, and murdered his entire family, that wasn't him who did it, he says, but something . . . someone . . . who got inside his body and took over. I just couldn't stop, says DeFeo.

Was DeFeo a suitable vehicle for spirit possession? The facts of my investigation strongly suggest it. DeFeo himself doesn't believe in anything supernatural. He doesn't understand what got into him. Did he massacre his family in cold blood, or under the influence of a power from beyond this dimension?

From the outset there were strange aspects to the case: nobody seems to have heard the shots which killed six people . . . how was it that none of the victims resisted or ran out of the murderer's way? Did they in fact not hear the shots either?

At DeFeo's trial, two eminent psychiatrists differed sharply about the state of the murderer's sanity: Dr. Schwartz considers DeFeo psychotic at the time of the murder, while Dr. Zolan holds him fully responsible for what he did. Rumors to the effect that DeFeo had first drugged his family's food (which would have explained their seeming apathy) proved groundless. The mystery remained even though DeFeo's sentence was clear: twenty-five years to life on each of the six counts of murder in the second degree, served consecutively—as if that mattered . . . over and over DeFeo repeated the same story: yes, he had killed his family, and felt no remorse over it. . . . but no, he didn't know why. Something . . . someone had gotten inside his person and forced him to shoot . . . going from bedroom to bedroom at 3 A.M. and exterminating the same parents, brothers and sisters he had lovingly embraced at a birthday party in the house a scant two months before the crime . . . whatever had gotten into DeFeo surely knew no mercy.

On January 15, 1977 I brought reputable trance medium Ethel Johnson Meyers to the house on Ocean Avenue, along with a psychic photographer to investigate what was shaping up as a case of suspected possession. Although Mrs. Meyers hadn't the slightest notion where she was or why I had brought her there, she immediately stated. . . . "Whoever lives here is going to be the victim of all the anger . . . the blind fierceness . . . this is Indian burial ground, sacred to them." As she was gradually slipping into trance, I asked why the Indian spirits were so angry.

"A white person got to digging around and dug up a skeleton . . ." She described a long-jawed Indian whose influence she felt in the house.

"People get to fighting with each other and they don't know why . . . they're driven to it because they are taken over by him." According to Mrs. Meyers, the long-ago misdeed of a white settler is still being avenged, every white man on the spot is an enemy, and when a catalyst moves there, he becomes a perfect vehicle for possession . . . like Ronald DeFeo.

"I see a dark young man wandering around at night . . . like in a trance . . . goes berserk . . . a whole family is involved . . ." the medium said and a shiver went up my spine. She had tuned right into the terrible past of the house.

When the pictures taken by the psychic photographer were developed on the spot, some of them showed strange haloes exactly where the bullets had struck . . . my camera jammed even though it had been working perfectly just before and was fine again the minute we left the house on Ocean Avenue . . . a house totally empty of life as we know it and yet filled with the shades of those who have passed on yet linger for they know not where to go. . . .

All sorts of charlatans had been to the house attracted by cheap publicity . . . until the new owners had enough. They knew all about the phenomena first-hand and eventually a best-selling book was based upon their experiences . . . embellished, enlarged and elaborated upon . . . but that is another kind of story. The real story was clear: 112 Ocean Avenue had been a psychically active location for perhaps two centuries . . . the phenomena ranging from footsteps and doors opening by themselves to the apparitions of figures that dissolve into thin air are well attested poltergeist manifestations, phenomena observed in literally thousands of similar cases all over the world . . . grist for the mills of the parapsychologist who knows there is no such thing as the supernatural, only facets of human personality transcending the old boundaries of conventional psychology . . . DeFeo had painted a little room in the basement red, because the color pleased him. The room he used as a kind of toolshed. An 18th century owner of the spot allegedly practiced witchcraft: add it all up, and enter the devil . . . DeFeo Sr. was a devoutly religious man who believed the devil was in the house, but his son left the house the minute the priest his father had called moved in.

When all the Satanic fallout had settled, I decided to investigate with the result that the real Amityville story began to emerge. What happened at Amityville could have happened anywhere in the world where passions are spent and human lives terminated by violence. The residue of the great crime lingers on even as the vehicle of possession gropes for an explanation of his true status. Young DeFeo is not a believer in things that go bump in the night, nor does he fear either God or the devil. But as he awaits still another interminable day in his cell at Dannemora prison, Ronald DeFeo cannot help wondering about the stranger within, the force that made him commit what he considers impossible crimes. He could have killed his father in an argument, perhaps, he concedes, but not his mother, not the children.

DeFeo may never get an answer he can live with, but he is young and may yet see the day when some future owner of that house has his innings with the Unknown. For that day will surely come. I've tried to exorcise the angry entity in the house, and though I have frequently succeeded in such cases, so much accumulated hatred is too powerful a reservoir to simply fade away. But in the end, we all get justice, one way or another.

52
THE STENTON HOUSE, CINCINNATI

I n one of the quietest and most elegant sections of old Cincinnati, where ghosts and hauntings are rarely whispered about, stands a lovely Victorian mansion built around 1850 in what was then a wealthy suburb of the city.

The house was brought to my attention some years ago by John S. of Clifton, a descendant of one of the early Dutch families who settled Cincinnati, and himself a student of the paranormal. The owners at that time were the Stenton family, or rather, of one of the apartments in the mansion, for it had long been subdivided into a number of apartments lived in by various people.

Soon after they had taken up residence in the old house, the Stentons were startled by noises, as if someone were walking in the hall, and when they checked, there was never anyone about who could have caused the walking. Then, two weeks after they had moved in, and always at exactly the same time, 2:10 A.M., they would hear the noise of a heavy object hitting the marble floor—of course there was nothing that could have caused it.

Shortly thereafter, while Mrs. Stenton and her father were doing some research work in the flat, someone softly called out her name, Marilyn. Both heard it. What really upset them was the sound of arguing voices coming from the area of the ceiling in their bedroom: Mrs. Stenton had the impression that there were a group of young girls up there!

But the most dramatic event was to transpire a couple of weeks later. Someone had entered the bedroom, and as she knew she was alone, her family being in other parts of the house, she was frightened, especially when she saw what appeared to be a misty figure—as soon as she had made eye contact with it, the

The Stenten house in Cincinnati, Ohio was the place of two suicides in the last century: disturbances have been observed ranging from footsteps and doors opening by themselves to apparitions.

figure shot out of the room, through the French doors leading to a studio, and whilst doing so, the misty shape managed to knock the Venetian blinds on the doors, causing them to sway back and forth!

Shortly before I visited Cincinnati to deal with this case, Mrs. Stenton had another eerie experience. It was winter and had been snowing the night before. When Mrs. Stenton stepped out onto their porch, she immediately noticed a fresh set of footprints on the porch, heading *away* from the house!

The house was built in 1850, originally as a large private home; later it became a girls' school and much later became an apartment house of sorts. The Stenton's apartment is the largest in the house, encompassing seven rooms.

When I looked into the case I discovered some additional details. In 1880, a young man of the Henry family had committed suicide in the house by shooting himself, and after the family moved, the house could not be sold for a long time. It became known as being haunted and was boarded up. Finally, a girls' school, the Ealy School, bought it in 1900.

Other tenants had also encountered unusual phenomena, ranging from "presences," to noises of objects hitting floors, and footsteps following one around when no one was, in fact, doing so. Even the dog owned by one of the tenants would under no condition enter the area of the disturbances and would put up a fearsome howl.

But the item most likely to have an answer to the goings-on came to me by talking to some of the oldsters in the area: one of the young girls in the school was said to have hanged herself upstairs, above the Stenton's apartment. Was it her ghost or that of young Henry who could not leave well enough alone?

53

THE GHOST ON EL CENTRO

hen Mr. and Mrs. C. moved from France to Los Angeles in the 1960's, they did not figure on moving into a haunted house, but that is exactly what they did. With their daughters, they took an old one-story house built in the Spanish style, on El Centro Avenue, a quiet section of the city.

One of the daughters, Lilliane had married shortly before their arrival, and the second daughter, Nicole, decided to have her own place, so it was Mr. and Mrs. C. and their third daughter, Martine, who actually lived in the house. The dining room had been turned into a bedroom for Martine, leaving the master bedroom to the parents.

On her first night in the house, Mrs. C., who is very psychic, had the distinct impression there was someone observing her, someone she could not see. Martine, too, felt very uncomfortable but the business of settling in took precedence over their concern for the next few days.

However, strong impressions of a presence continued night after night. They were never "alone." There was a noise in the kitchen, and Mrs. C. thought her husband had gotten up in the middle of the night to get something—but there he was, fast asleep in bed. Instead, a strange man was standing between their two beds, and worse yet, she could see right through him! She gave out a startling cry and the apparition vanished instantly.

She discussed the matter with her daughters who had lived in the apartment before their arrival: it then became clear that the girls, too, had been bothered by ghostly manifestations. They had tried to deal with it by lighting a candle every night. But apparently it did not help at all.

During the following days, the hauntings continued. The girls, too, had seen a male ghost between the beds. But now the mother saw a woman's apparition, and it was decided to seek the help of a competent medium. This turned out to be Brenda Crenshaw, who made contact with the entities. She reported that the "problem"

consisted of the fact a young couple who had formerly occupied the apartment, had committed suicide in it.

When the family checked this out with the appropriate records, it turned out to be correct. But now what? The idea of continuing to share the place with the ghost couple was not at all appealing to them. Mrs. C. decided to pray for the release of the ghosts and did so relentlessly for several weeks. One night, there was the young man again, as if to acknowledge her efforts. Then he vanished, and the apartment has been quiet ever since.

This pleasant looking house on El Centro Street in Los Angeles was the site of a suicide by a young couple years ago. Later residents have encountered their restless, unhappy ghosts.

54

A REVOLUTIONARY GHOST

n Byberry Road in Somerton, Pennsylvania, not far from Philadelphia, stands a charming little house built in 1732. When I visited it in the company of the late medium Sybil Leek, it belonged to the R.'s who had called on me to do something about that Colonial soldier who thought it was still his place.

Set back somewhat from the road, it boasts three floors, and the R.'s had furnished it with a keen sense of style. Perhaps that, more than anything else, contributed to the Colonial ghost's presence, since he must have felt very much at home in the place.

Now Mrs. R., being Irish, was no stranger to psychic experiences: when she was but fourteen, and reading in bed one night, the door opened and her brother Paul stood there which caused Mrs. R. to duck under the covers inasmuch as Paul had been dead for eight years.

When the R.'s moved into the old house, they soon realized they weren't exactly alone in it. Both heard footsteps when no one was walking about, doors would open by themselves, and cold air blasts would be felt without apparent reason. At first, she thought her children were playing pranks but she soon found out this was not so, the children being fast asleep in their respective beds.

It got so that "someone" unseen would open the door for her as if to accommodate her. One way or another, the doors would simply not stay shut. A rocking chair would start up by itself. A week before our visit, a rotisserie rack came sailing down the stairs toward her and had she not ducked quickly it would have hit her: clearly, our coming was not viewed enthusiastically by the ghost.

My first visit had convinced me that a trance medium was required to make contact with this ghost, so when I returned this time, I had Sybil Leek with me.

As soon as Sybil had relaxed sufficiently, she went into a state of deep trance and the ghost was able to communicate with me. It turned out his name was John Ross and the house had been a "meeting place," in 1744. Fact is, the house was a Quaker "meeting house," according to records I checked later.

A Colonial officer who lost his way during the revolutionary war is the cause of a remarkable haunting at this lovely suburban house at Somerset, Pennsylvania.

And why was Captain John Ross hanging out in this house, I wanted to know. He confided, through Sybil, that he was all for peace, and that he served in the 25th cavalry regiment. He spoke of a battle in this spot, and having been hurt. He was waiting "for them" to fetch him, but he liked the house because it was "a meeting place to pray." It appears the man was a Quaker and he was lost, having been killed in battle. Later, I was able to trace John Ross in the Regimental records of the time. Some of the fellow officers he named during the trance, also proved to have served during that period when Revolutionaries and Tories fighting one another often belonged to the same family, for, like it or not, the American Revolutionary War was less a war of liberation than a Civil War between those seeking independence and those preferring to stay part of the British Empire.

55
THE SAN FRANCISCO GHOST BRIDE

ot far from the Fairmont Hotel on Nob Hill, San Francisco, where the popular television series *Hotel* was taped, is a spot considered haunted by many. Here on California Street, in front of an average apartment house going back some years, the ghost of Flora Sommerton walks. Many have seen the girl, dressed in her bridal gown, walking right through living people and totally oblivious of them, and they, of her. Some years ago Mrs. Gwen H., a lady I worked with on a number of cases, was riding up the hill with a friend, in a cable car. Both ladies saw the strange girl in her bridal gown walking fast as if trying to get away from something—or someone.

Which is exactly what she tried to do. Flora Sommerton, a San Francisco debutante, was eighteen when she disappeared from her family's Nob Hill mansion one night in 1876. It was a major society scandal at the time: Flora simply had refused to marry the young man her parents had picked for her to marry.

Flora never came back nor was she ever found, despite a vast search and huge reward offered for her return or information leading to her. The years went by and eventually the matter was forgotten. Flora's parents also died and it was not until 1926 when the truth finally came out. That year Flora died in a flophouse in Butte, Montana, still dressed in her bridal gown. Ever since, she has been seen walking up Nob Hill desperately trying to escape an unwanted marriage.

If you will slowly walk up California Street, late at night when there is little traffic, perhaps you too might run into the wide-eyed lass from 1876 and if you do, be sure to tell her it is time to let go, and that she is finally free.

56
THE RESTLESS GHOST OF BERGENVILLE

rs. Ethel Meyers, who has frequently accompanied me on ghost-hunting expeditions, heard from friends living in Bergen County, New Jersey, about some unusual happenings at their very old house. Eventually the "safari for ghost" was organized, and Mr. B., the master of the house, picked us up in his car and drove us to Bergen County. The house turned out to be a beautifully preserved pre-Revolutionary house set within an enclosure of tall trees and lawns.

The building had been started in 1704, I later learned, and the oldest portion was the right wing; the central portion was added in the latter part of the eighteenth century, and the final, frontal portion was built from old materials about fifty years ago, carefully preserving the original style of the house. The present owners had acquired it about a year ago from a family who had been in possession for several generations. The house was then empty, and the B.'s refurbished it completely in excellent taste with antiques of the period.

After they moved into the house, they slept for a few days on a mattress on the enclosed porch, which skirted the west wing of the house. Their furniture had not yet arrived, and they didn't mind roughing it for a short while. It was summer and not too cool.

In the middle of the night, Mrs. B. suddenly awoke with the uncanny feeling that there was *someone else* in the house, besides her husband and herself. She got up and walked toward the corridorlike extension of the enclosed porch running along the back of the house. There she clearly distinguished the figure of a man seemingly white, with a beard, wearing what she described as "something ruffly white." She had the odd sensation that this man belonged to a much earlier period than the present. The light was good enough to see the man clearly for about five minutes, in which she was torn between fear of the intruder and curiosity. Finally she approached him, and saw him *literally dissolve before her very eyes!* At the same time, she had the odd sensation that the stranger came to look *them* over, wondering what they were doing in *his* house! Mrs. B., a celebrated actress and choreographer, is not a scoffer, nor is she easily susceptible. Ghosts to her are something one can discuss intelligently. Since her husband shared this view, they inquired of the former owner about any possible hauntings.

"I've never heard of any or seen any," Mr. S. told them, "but my daughter-in-law has never been able to sleep in the oldest part of the house. Said there was too much going on there. Also, one of the neighbors claims he saw *something*."

Mr. S. wasn't going to endanger his recent real estate transaction with too many ghostly tales. The B.'s thanked him and settled down to life in their colonial house.

But they soon learned that theirs was a busy place indeed. Both are artistic and very intuitive, and they soon became aware of the presence of unseen forces.

One night Mrs. B. was alone at home, spending the evening in the upper story of the house. There was nobody downstairs. Suddenly she heard the downstairs front door open and shut. There was no mistaking the very characteristic and complex sound of the opening of this ancient lock! Next, she heard footsteps, and sighed with relief. Apparently her husband had returned much earlier than expected. Quickly, she rushed down the stairs to welcome him. There was nobody there. There was no one in front of the door. All she found was the cat in a strangely excited state!

Sometime after, Mr. B. came home. For his wife these were anxious hours of waiting. He calmed her as best he could, having reservations about the whole incident. Soon these doubts were to be dispelled completely.

This time Mrs. B. was away and Mr. B. was alone in the downstairs part of the house. The maid was asleep in her room, the B.'s child fast asleep upstairs. It was a peaceful evening, and Mr. B. decided to have a snack. He found himself in the kitchen, which is located at the western end of the downstairs part of the house, *when he suddenly heard a car drive up*. Next, there were the distinct sounds of the front door opening and closing again. As he rushed to the front door, he heard the dog bark furiously. But again, there was no one either inside or outside the house!

Mr. B., a star and director, and as rational a man as could be, wondered if he had imagined these things. But he knew he had not. What he had heard were clearly the noises of an arrival. While he was still trying to sort out the meaning of all this, another strange thing happened.

A few evenings later, he found himself alone in the downstairs living room, when he heard carriage wheels outside grind to a halt. He turned his head toward the door, wondering who it might be at this hour. The light was subdued, but good enough to read by. He didn't have to wait long. A short, husky man walked into the room *through* the closed door; then, without paying attention to Mr. B., turned and walked out into the oldest part of the house, again *through a closed door!*

"What did he look like to you?" I asked.

"He seemed dotted, as if he were made of thick, solid dots, and he wore a long coat, the kind they used to wear around 1800. He probably was the same man my wife encountered."

"You think he is connected with the oldest part of the house?"

"Yes, I think so. About a year ago I played some very old lute music, the kind popular in the eighteenth century, in there—and something happened to the atmosphere in the room. As if someone were listening quietly and peacefully."

But it wasn't always as peaceful in there. A day before our arrival, Mrs. B.

had lain down, trying to relax. But she could not stay in the old room. "There was someone there," she said simply.

The B.'s weren't the only ones to hear and see ghosts. Last summer, two friends of the B.'s were visiting them, and everybody was seated in the living room, when in plain view of all, the screen door to the porch opened and closed again *by its own volition!* Needless to add, the friends didn't stay long.

Only a day before our visit, another friend had tried to use the small washroom in the oldest part of the house. Suddenly, he felt chills coming on and rushed out of the room, telling Mrs. B. that "someone was looking at him."

At this point, dinner was ready, and a most delicious repast it was. Afterwards we accompanied the B.'s into the oldest part of their house, a low-ceilinged room dating back to the year 1704. Two candles provided the only light. Mrs. Meyers got into a comfortable chair, and gradually drifted into trance.

"Marie . . . Catherine . . . who calls?" she mumbled.

"Who is it?" I inquired.

"Pop . . . live peacefully . . . love. . . ."

What is your name?" I wanted to know.

"Achabrunn. . . ."

I didn't realize it at the time, but a German family named Achenbach had built the house and owned it for several generations. Much later still, I found out that one of the children of the builder had been called Marian.

I continued my interrogation.

"Who rules this country?"

"The Anglish. George."

"What year is this?"

"56. 1756."

"When did you stay here?"

"Always. Pop. My house. *You* stay with *me*."

Then the ghost spoke haltingly of his family, his children, of which he had nine, three of whom had gone away.

"What can we do for you?" I said, hoping to find the reason for the many disturbances.

"Yonder over side hill, hillock, three buried . . . flowers there."

"Do you mean," I said, "that we should put flowers on these graves?"

The medium seemed excited.

"*Ach Gott, ja, machs gut.*" With this the medium crossed herself.

"What is your name?" I asked again.

"Oterich . . . Oblich . . ." The medium seemed hesitant as if the ghost were searching his memory for his own name. Later, I found that the name given was pretty close to that of another family having a homestead next door.

The ghost continued.

"She lady . . . I not good. I very stout heart, I look up to good-blood lady I make her good . . . Kathrish, holy lady, I worship lady . . . they rest on hill too, with three. . . ."

After the seance, I found a book entitled *Pre-Revolutionary Dutch Houses in Northern New Jersey and New York*. It was here that I discovered the tradition that a poor shepherd from Saxony married a woman above his station, and built this very house. The year 1756 was correct.

But back to my interrogation. "Why don't you rest on the hillock?"

"I take care of . . . four . . . hillock . . . Petrish. Ladian, Annia, Kathrish. . . ."

Then, as if taking cognizance of us, he added—"To care for you, that's all I want."

Mrs. B. nodded and said softly, "You're always welcome here."

Afterward, I found that there were indeed some graves on the hill beyond the house. The medium now pointed toward the rear of the house, and said, "Gate . . . we put intruders there, he won't get up any more. Gray Fox made trouble, Indian man, I keep him right there."

"Are there any passages?"

"Yeah. Go dig through. When Indian come, they no find."

"Where?"

"North hillock, still stone floor there, ends here."

From Mr. B. I learned that underground passages are known to exist between this house and the so-called "Slave House," across the road.

The ghost then revealed that his wife's father, an Englishman, had built the passage, and that stores were kept in it along with Indian bones.

"Where were you born?" I inquired.

"Here. Bergenville."

Bergenville proved to be the old name of the township.

I then delicately told him that this was 1960. He seemed puzzled, to say the least.

"In 1756 I was sixty-five years old. I am not 204 years older?"

At this point, the ghost recognized the women's clothing the medium was wearing, and tore at them. I explained how we were able to "talk" to him. He seemed pacified.

"You'll accept my maize, my wine, my whiskey. . . ."

I discovered that maize and wine staples were the mainstays of the area at that period. I also found that Indian wars on a small scale were still common in this area in the middle 1700's. Moreover, the ghost referred to the "gate" as being in the *rear* of the house. This proved to be correct, for what is now the back of the house was then its front, facing the road.

Suddenly the ghost withdrew and after a moment another person, a woman, took over the medium. She complained bitterly that the Indians had taken one of her children, whose names she kept rattling off. Then she too withdrew, and Mrs. Meyers returned to her own body, none the worse for her experiences, none of which, incidentally, she remembered.

Shortly afterward, we returned to New York. It was as if we had just come from another world. Leaving the poplar-lined road behind us, we gradually re-entered the world of gasoline and dirt that is the modern city.

Nothing further has been reported from the house in Bergen County, but I am sure the ghost, whom Mrs. B. had asked to stay as long as he wished, is still there. There is of course no further need to bang doors, to call attention to his lonely self. *They know he is there with them.*

57
THE GHOSTLY STAGECOACH INN

ot far from Ventura, at Thousand Oaks, a few yards back from the main road, stands an old stagecoach inn, now run as a museum; between 1952 and 1965, while in the process of being restored to its original appearance, it also served as a gift shop under the direction of a Mr. and Mrs. M. who had sensed the presence of a female ghost in the structure.

The house has 19 rooms and an imposing frontage with columns running from the floor to the roof. There is a balcony in the central portion, and all windows have shutters, in the manner of the middle nineteenth century. Surrounded by trees until a few years ago, it has been moved recently to a new position to make room for the main road running through here. Nevertheless, its grandeur has not been affected by the move.

During the stagecoach days, bandits were active in this area. The inn had been erected because of the Butterfield Mail route, which was to have gone through the Conejo Valley on the way to St. Louis. The Civil War halted this plan, and the routing was changed to go through the Santa Clara Valley.

I investigated the stagecoach inn with Mrs. Gwen Hinzie and Sybil Leek. Up the stairs to the left of the staircase Sybil noticed one of the particularly haunted rooms. She felt that a man named Pierre Devon was somehow connected with the building. Since the structure was still in a state of disrepair, with building activities going on all around us, the task of walking up the stairs was not only a difficult one but also somewhat dangerous, for we could not be sure that the wooden structure would not collapse from our weight. We stepped very gingerly. Sybil seemed to know just where to turn as if she had been there before. Eventually, we ended up in a little room to the left of the stairwell. It must have been one of the smaller rooms, a "single" in today's terms.

Sybil complained of being cold all over. The man, Pierre Devon, had been killed in that room, she insisted, sometime between 1882 and 1889.

She did not connect with the female ghost. However, several people living in the area have reported the presence of a tall stranger who could only be seen out of the corner of an eye, never for long. Pungent odors, perfume of a particularly heavy kind, also seem to waft in and out of the structure.

Like inns in general, this one may have more undiscovered ghosts hanging on to the spot. Life in nineteenth-century wayside inns did not compare favorably with life in today's Hilton. Some people going to these stagecoach inns for a night's rest never woke up to see another day.